THE VIETNAM WAR
The Early Days

The
MILITARY HISTORY
of the
UNITED STATES

Christopher Chant

THE VIETNAM WAR
The Early Days

MARSHALL CAVENDISH
NEW YORK · LONDON · TORONTO · SYDNEY

NOV 6 '92

Library Edition Published 1992

© Marshall Cavendish Limited 1992

Published by
Marshall Cavendish Corporation
2415 Jerusalem Avenue
PO Box 587
North Bellmore
New York 11710

Series created by Graham Beehag Book Design

Series Editor	Maggi McCormick
Consultant Editors	James R. Arnold
	Roberta Wiener
Sub Editor	Julie Cairns
Designer	Graham Beehag
Illustrators	John Batchelor
	Steve Lucas
	Terry Forest
	Colette Brownrigg
Indexer	Mark Dartford

Library of Congress Cataloging-in-Publication Data

Chant, Christopher.
    The Military History of the United States / Christopher Chant –
Library ed.
        p. cm.
    Includes bibliographical references and index.
    Summary: Surveys the wars that have directly influenced the
    United States., from the Revolutionary War through the Cold War.
    ISBN 1-85435-363-2 ISBN 1-85435-361-9 (set)
    1. United States - History, Military - Juvenile literature.
    [1. United States - History, Military.] 1. Title.
    t181.C52 1991
    973 - dc20   90 - 19547
                                                        CIP
                                                        AC

Printed in Singapore by Times Offset PTE Ltd
Bound in the United States

The publishers wish to thank the following organizations
who have supplied photographs:

The National Archives, Washington. United States
Navy, United States Marines, United States Army,
United States Air Force, Department of Defense,
Library of Congress, The Smithsonian Institution.

The publishers gratefully thank the U.S. Army Military
History Institute, Carlisle Barracks, PA. for the use of
archive material for the following witness accounts:

Page 57
Handbook for U.S. Forces in Vietnam, Military
Assistance Command, Vietnam, 1965

Page 74
Why Pleime, by ARVN Major General Vinh-Loc
(Pleiku, 1966).

Page 106-107
Cedar Falls Junction City: A Turning Point,
by Lieutenant General Bernard William Rogers,
Department of the Army.

Contents

Their experience of World War I and World War II had led most Americans to a belief, unreasoned but nonetheless strong, that their armed forces could and would produce decisive results. The Korean War shattered this belief; three years of bitter fighting had yielded only a battlefield stalemate that was reflected in the eventual end of the war – an armistice rather than the surrender of the enemy. This led to a degree of frustration in the armed forces and among the American people, but did not alter the general relief that was felt at the end of this comparatively small but bloody war. Even so, the feeling was that the armistice negotiated at Panmunjom was only a truce that would in all probability be only temporary in the continuing struggle between the United States and the U.S.S.R. The signing of the Panmunjom armistice ended the shooting, but just as surely marked a transition back to international tensions of the "Cold War."

The Korean War had demonstrated with absolute clarity that the United States was the only country that possessed both the will and the strength to resist communist expansion. The war had also revealed with alarming sureness that an era in American diplomatic and military thinking had ended. For some time, the country had worked on the basis of several allies bearing the main weight of the initial fighting as the United States prepared for war, but this no longer held true. If the United States was to continue its policy of containing the threat of communist expansion, the nation would now have to use its own forces for the

Throughout the 1950s, the U.S. Army made determined efforts to increase the combat efficiency of its forces, but it was virtually impossible to reconcile the needs of a modern high-technology army with short-term draftees. This high-tech machine is the turret on an M50 Ontos, a specialized tank destroyer whose traversing turret accommodated on each side an elevating trio of 106-mm (4·2-inch) recoilless rifles.

task right from the beginning. Large standing forces would have to be maintained; their great cost would have to be borne, as there appeared little chance during 1953 and the following years that diplomacy alone could achieve worthwhile results.

Acceptance that powerful armed forces were essential in the conduct of American diplomacy at the international level was now necessary. This assent demanded a radical change in the U.S. concept of itself. Up to now, the country had mobilized only in response to a specific and developing threat of war. Its wars had for the most part been fought almost as crusades which enjoyed strong emotional and moral support from the population at large. After the Korean War, the task of combating communism demanded that the American people accept the sustained possibility of military action to check an opponent who regarded military action as a simple extension of international politics.

Perhaps surprisingly, given the alteration of the emotional balance and the economic burden involved, the American people agreed with little objection to the burden of leading what was very rapidly becoming known as the free world.

Policy under the Eisenhower Administration

Once the fighting in Korea ended, the administration of President Dwight D. Eisenhower could start the constructive process of planning the United States' linked diplomatic and military strategy, and of determining the size and nature of the armed forces needed to carry out that strategy. The two main factors that the president and his advisers had to bear in mind were the worldwide nature of U.S. commitments, and the need to cut defense spending for economic reasons. The result was an increased emphasis on nuclear weapons, both strategic and tactical, to be delivered by aircraft. This capitalized on the American lead over the Soviets in technological matters, allowed the maintenance of forces that were comparatively small in manpower terms, and

yet gave the United States a truly global reach with powerful weapons.

Within the context of the United States' reliance on nuclear air power, the Korean War was seen as an oddity. From now on, U.S. forces would be committed to a major land war against communist forces only as a matter of last resort. The administration's thinking was neatly encapsulated by John Foster Dulles, the Secretary of State, in the following way: "The basic decision was to depend primarily upon a greater capacity to retaliate, instantly, by means and at places of our choosing. Now the Department of Defense and the Joint Chiefs of Staff can shape our military establishment to fit what is our policy, instead of having to try to be ready to meet the enemy's many choices. That permits a selection of military means instead of a multiplication of means. As a result, it is now possible to get, and share, more basic security at less cost."

The Doctrine of Massive Retaliation

The effort to regain the strategic initiative by means of strong response to any given situation was a deliberate attempt to raise the threshold of war and therefore to make war less likely, as the lowest stakes were that much higher. The U.S. response, known as the doctrine of mas-

As Secretary of State, John Foster Dulles was largely responsible for the American policy of "massive retaliation," in which even small-scale Soviet aggression would be met by an all-out American counterattack.

Dwight D. Eisenhower
For further references see pages
11, 14, 17, 23, 24

The 7th Fleet was permanently deployed in the western Pacific as part of the U.S. presence in this strategically vital area. The fleet has always contained a representative spread of the navy's latest fighting ships and amphibious warfare vessels. This is the U.S.S. *Princeton, an* amphibious assault ship which was converted from a World War II carrier and finally deleted in 1970.

sive retaliation, relied most heavily on its nuclear superiority The nuclear deterrence policy lay at the heart of American defense thinking and planning: the threat posed by massive retaliation would deter the U.S.S.R. from pushing the United States and her allies too far.

After all previous American wars, the industrial basis for the military effort was dismantled. After 1953, this did not happen. The constant threat posed by the U.S.S.R., and the rapid development of high-technology weapons, made rearmament a continuous process and demanded that significant forces be maintained as the basis on which rapid wartime expansion could be undertaken if deterrence failed. The American armed forces therefore assumed a new form from the mid-1950s. The U.S. Air Force

strengthened its strategic bomber force and began developing long-range ballistic missiles. The navy devoted a great part of its effort to perfecting the Polaris submarine-launched ballistic missile, and the army made a successful attempt to create the first generation of battlefield nuclear weapons.

Inter-service Disputes

The type of nuclear warfare now being envisaged had never been waged, of course, and the absence of experience meant developing new warfare on the basis of abstract theory rather than real experience. National defense guidelines had to be general rather than specific, and inevitably there were disputes

A marine practices the apparently simple, but actually highly skilled task of camouflage. Such dexterity was vital in the close fighting country that the marines found in Vietnam.

about the numbers and types of forces needed. This placed a great burden on the secretary of defense, who had to adjudicate in the disagreements between the military leaders. In the circumstances, it was hardly surprising that the House Appropriations Committee decided that "Each service, it would seem, is striving to develop and acquire an arsenal of weapons complete in itself to carry out any and all possible missions."

The annual military budget was divided by service rather than by mission, so the distribution often resulted in considerable bitterness between the services. From the mid-1950s, the air force's allocation grew considerably as the service procured new bombers and missiles for its nuclear role: the 1955 appropriation of slightly more than $34 billion, for example, included $15.6 billion for the air force, but only $9.7 billion and $8.85 billion respectively for the navy and army. The capability to wage a conventional war declined sharply, and the doctrine of massive retaliation came to be distrusted by the army and navy, the chief protagonists of conventional war.

When he retired as Army Chief of Staff in June 1955, General Matthew B. Ridgway expressed this distrust most forcefully. In Ridgway's opinion, the development of Soviet nuclear capability would result in a situation of parity in which neither side enjoyed a clearcut superiority. The Soviets would therefore be able to shift a sizable part of their planning effort to the worldwide manufacture of situations in which nuclear weapons could not be used. Should this happen, Ridgway

Maxwell D. Taylor
For further references
see pages
31, 40, 43, 45, 47, 48,
52, 56, 57, 68

concluded, the conventional forces of the United States would not be strong enough to deal with even the non-nuclear threat posed by the Soviets. As Ridgway concluded: "The present United States preoccupation with preparations for general war has limited the military means available for cold war to those which are essentially by-products or leftovers from the means available for general war."

A Plea for Balanced Forces

Ridgway's departing plea was thus for a more balanced composition of U.S. forces so that they could cope with either general or limited war. This point of view was also put forward by Ridgway's successor, General Maxwell D. Taylor, and by a large number of civilian advisers in the higher levels of the American defense establishment. For the rest of the 1950s, the forces, Congress, the universities, and the media were all forums for heated debate about the merits of general against limited war, conventional against nuclear war, and any number of intermediate steps between the two extremes. It was only in the later part of the decade, as the U.S.S.R.'s approaching nuclear parity with the United States became clearer, that some of the main proponents of nuclear war finally agreed that such a war would result in the mutual destruc-

tion of the U.S.S.R. and the United States, and that in these circumstances the nuclear option should become "the last and not the only recourse."

Even as these controversies continued in the United States, the existing nuclear strategy had exercised a great influence over U.S. foreign policy and the fundamental nature of her armed forces. During 1952 and 1953, the limited nature of the war in Korea had been reflected in the major development and expansion of the U.S. forces in Europe rather than the Far East. At the beginning of the Korean War, the army had just one division in Europe, but the possibility that the U.S.S.R. might use American preoccupation with Korea to undertake a European adventure became clear: by the end of the Korean War, there were five American divisions in Europe. Moreover, through the Mutual Defense Assistance Program, the U.S. had made a significant contribution to the strengthening of the forces deployed by other members of the North Atlantic Treaty Organization. During the period, NATO developed a "forward defense" strategy for defensive operations in western Germany as far east of the Rhine River as possible.

Reinforcement of Europe

In the mid-1950s, the situation in Europe changed considerably with the ending of the Korean War, the launch of a Soviet

During the 1950s, the forces made great strides in the development of guided missiles of all types and placed a considerable number in service. Resulting from a 1945 requirement for a surface-to-surface tactical missile, the Martin Matador was in essence a pilotless turbojet-powered airplane intended to deliver a 3,000-pound nuclear or conventional warhead over a range of 650 miles after launch with the aid of a powerful solid-propellant booster rocket. This Matador of the air force 11th Missile Squadron is seen on maneuvers at Fort Polk, Louisiana.

President Dwight D. Eisenhower talks with General Paul Ely, the chairman of the French chiefs of staff, and Admiral Arthur Radford, the chairman of the Joint Chiefs of Staff. Throughout its two terms, the Eisenhower administration sought to avoid entanglement in the legacy of French rule in Indochina.

diversionary peace movement in Europe, and the death of the Soviet dictator, Josef Stalin. These factors eased the high level of tension in Europe, and the U.S. and its allies thankfully welcomed the chance to slow the pace of military buildup on the continent, a program that had inflicted severe economic pain on the western European nations and, to a lesser extent, the United States. The slowing of the buildup reduced the flow of men and equipment to Europe and allowed a greater concentration on the alliance's war-fighting infrastructure such as airfields, supply depots, bridges able to support modern armored fighting vehicles, and signal communications. In the same period, the United States sought unsuccessfully to persuade its European allies to integrate their forces fully into the NATO structure and argued successfully for the rearmament of West Germany and its integration into NATO's military and political organization.

It was clear, however, that the Soviets and their satellites still enjoyed numerical superiority in Europe over the western European nations, even with American support. This imbalance, most marked in the all-important ground forces, resulted in a considerable American effort to develop tactical nuclear warheads that could be delivered by artillery projectiles and missiles. As these warheads became available, NATO contingency planning came to be based on the simple yet dangerous premise that any Soviet attack would be countered by nuclear weapons. These weapons were to be fired or delivered by equipment of the NATO alliance's European members, but their control remained exclusively an American prerogative. This was particularly irksome to several European countries, and was one reason why the United Kingdom and France decided to press ahead with the development of their own nuclear weapons and delivery systems free of U.S. control.

The Soviet Threat Increases

The pace of American military development was matched by the Soviet effort. The U.S.S.R. developed turbine-powered intercontinental bombers, and on August 12, 1953, surprised the world with the detonation of its first hydrogen bomb after an extraordinarily rapid research program. By the mid-1950s, the Soviets had a genuine strategic nuclear capability and were pressing ahead with the development of intercontinental ballistic missiles as well as tactical nuclear weapons. From 1955, the superpowers possessed nuclear arsenals capable of obliterating each other's cities and industries. In the summer of 1955, the two superpowers met at a summit conference in Geneva, Switzerland. It became clear then that each side recognized that the nuclear arms race was leading to the probability of mutual destruction rather than victory on either side. This recognition did not slow the pace of the superpowers' development of even greater nuclear capabilities, but as each saw that the other would not resort to nuclear war unless its very survival was threatened, the tension between relaxed.

In 1956 came clear evidence that the U.S.S.R. was modifying its strategic stance when the Soviet premier, Nikita Khrushchev, suggested that the communist and free worlds could coexist peacefully but competitively. In this way, Khrushchev made it clear that the U.S.S.R. would not back away from participation in or sponsorship of "wars of national liberation" against the nations of the free world. In short, the communists would carry on the struggle between communism and capitalism by all means other than a general war directly between the two superpowers.

To a certain extent, therefore, there was a modest thaw in the "Cold War." The United States knew, however, that this thaw could quickly re-freeze. It kept up its guard, including the completion in 1957 of a series of early warning radar warning stations. Undertaken with Canada, the DEW (Distant Early Warning) Line was built through Alaska and northern Canada to provide warning of Soviet bombers approaching North America via the optimum polar route. The DEW Line supplemented earlier radar installations in central and southern Canada; its capability enhanced radar picket aircraft, radar outposts in the Aleutian Islands, and a combination of radar towers and radar picket ships in the Atlantic.

Improved Defense Against Soviet Bombers

Responsibility for this network and its associated air defenses was entrusted to the Continental Air Defense Command, with the air force as executive agent. The air force's interceptor squadrons were

complemented by the army's surface-to-air missile system, whose first genuinely effective long-range weapon was the Nike Ajax.

For offensive purposes, the manned bomber still reigned supreme. Change was in the offing, though, in the form of the ballistic missile. The army's Jupiter and the air force's Thor were under development in the intermediate range bracket, and the air force's Atlas and Titan in the intercontinental range. Under an earlier agreement defining the services' roles and missions, the army was responsible for point defense and the air force for area defense, which led to an important jurisdictional dispute between the two services. On November 26, 1956, Secretary of Defense Charles E.

One of the most important lessons learned in World War II for amphibious operations was the need for saturation bombardment of the assault beach. This is the U.S.S. *St. Francis River*, a landing ship medium (rocket), during a typical bombardment.

Opposite Top: The mainstay of the U.S. Air Force's contribution to the American nuclear deterrent from the mid-1950s was the Boeing B-52 Stratofortress bomber. Though it was more vulnerable than long-range missiles, it had the advantages that it could be retargeted easily and could also be recalled. This example is seen releasing a "Hound dog" stand-off missile, a supersonic missile carrying a four-megaton thermonuclear warhead.

Opposite Bottom: The other side of the manned bomber equation was protection against Soviet aircraft of this type, and a limited but useful capability was provided by the Nike system. It was very expensive and led to offshoots such as the Nike Zeus, seen here in a test launch. The Nike Zeus was the United States' first antiballistic missile, but was only a limited success.

Wilson cut back the army's responsibility by giving the air force control of all missiles with a range of 200 miles (322 km) or more, though for obvious reasons the army was allowed to complete development of the Jupiter. At the same time, Wilson drastically cut back the army's planned aviation program.

The Emergence of the Long-range Missile

Shortly afterward, the U.S.S.R. spurred the United States to greater efforts by firing a clearly operational intercontinental ballistic missile. Then, on October 4, 1957, she launched into space the world's first artificial satellite, Sputnik 1. It was immediately clear that the U.S.S.R. had moved considerably ahead of the United States in booster technology, with far-reaching implications in the military sphere. An intensive program of research and development to reduce and then reverse the Soviets' advantage in this crucial element of strategic missile technology began, and the Minuteman intercontinental and Poseidon submarine-launched ballistic missiles were developed fairly rapidly. While they did not match contemporary Soviet missiles for size and weight, they

did offer comparable range, together with considerably greater accuracy as a result of their far more sophisticated guidance packages.

The missile race also brought up the question of whether or not the U.S. needed to maintain military bases and garrisons in a large number of overseas spots. As part of its decision to surround China and the U.S.S.R. with offensive weapons during the harshest period of the "Cold War," the United States had negotiated defense agreements with a number of countries that allowed aircraft and missile bases in areas around China and the U.S.S.R. The advent of the long-range missile threw the need for these bases into question. The rising cost of establishing and maintaining such bases had begun to worry Congress and the administration, and the Government began to think of abandoning these bases as soon as long-range missiles were available in adequate numbers.

Renewed Possibility of Limited War

As U.S. commitments to support friendly nations and implement the nation's global military strength extended around

power soon began to unbalance the composition of the American forces. In 1953, the army had a $13-billion slice of the $34-billion military appropriation for its strength of slightly more than 1,500,000 men and 20 first-line divisions (eight in the Far East, five in Europe, and seven in the United States).

The National Security Council then fixed lower appropriation and manpower ceilings for the services after the Korean War, and the Joint Chiefs of Staff responded with a plan to cut overall strength by 600,000 men over the next four years. The air force and navy were faced with some manpower losses, but the army faced the most severe cuts. By 1958, the cuts had been implemented; the army had shrunk to slightly less than 900,000 men and 15 first-line divisions (two in South Korea, five in Europe, seven in the United States, and one in Hawaii), for which $9 billion was allocated out of a total military appropriation of just over $41 billion.

Further Inter-services Disputes

In a climate of forced cuts, stringent budgetary ceilings, a complex international situation, and a rapidly developing technology that seemed to make advanced weapons obsolete as soon as they were developed, the constant dispute between the services about funding, overall strategy, and force levels caused Congress considerable concern. On April 16, 1958, Eisenhower detailed plans for a major reorganization, with the fourfold objectives of stopping "unworthy and sometimes costly [inter-service] bickering," assuring "clear-cut civilian responsibility, unified strategic planning and completely unified commands," halting "inefficiency and needless duplication," and guaranteeing "safety and solvency." The plan was changed by Congress before being approved in August as the Reorganization Act; but even so, the president achieved his primary objectives of strengthening the position and authority of the secretary of defense in relation to other departments, creating a limited general staff organization to serve the needs of

A test launch of the Atlas intercontinental ballistic missile from Vandenberg Air Force Base in California reveals the huge size of these liquid-propellant missiles. Perched on the nose is the reentry vehicle carrying the warhead.

the world, it became clear that American forces were more likely to become involved in limited wars than in a general conflict. Yet the military budget since the end of the Korean War had been based on the assumption of general rather than limited war. President Eisenhower was also making strenuous efforts to reduce military spending from the high levels reached during the Korean War. Though budget reductions seemed laudable, astute commentators worried that the defense establishment was being tailored to meet the administration's budgetary ceilings rather than the evolving military needs of the country. Emphasis on strategic air

The core of the U.S. Navy's capabilities in the 1950s and early 1960s rested with its force of large aircraft carriers. This is the U.S.S. *Kitty Hawk* refueling two of her escorting destroyers at sea. Note the carrier's angled flight deck, complete with two launcher catapults. The availability of this angled-out section allowed aircraft to land as others were launched from the two catapults on the straight bow section.

the Joint Chiefs of Staff, and reassigning responsibility for the service elements of the unified commands to the service secretaries and the chiefs of staff.

The 1958 Reorganization Act

From now on, the practice of using the military departments as executive agencies for operations was abolished. Virtually all of the active forces were placed under the control of the unified command controlled by the president and secretary of defense via the Joint Chiefs of Staff. The secretary of defense had greater authority to shift tasks between the services. At the level of the Joint Chiefs of Staff, the Joint Staff was made larger, but was not allowed to organize or operate as an overall general staff for the armed services as a whole. And the Joint Chiefs of Staff were authorized to delegate some of their routine administrative tasks to the vice chiefs.

Under this reorganization, individual services were still responsible for training, equipping, and organizing the forces needed by the unified commands, and for developing the weapons that would be required by these forces. The individual services retained control of all units not specifically assigned to unified commands and had to provide logistical

John F. Kennedy
For further references
see pages
17, 31, 39

support for all their forces, whether or not they were allocated to unified commands.

The 1958 reorganization marked the practical end of the military departments' traditional role, and the Joint Chiefs of Staff and the unified commands assumed the dominant position in the American military establishment.

By the time this organizational revision was ordered, the services themselves had already modified their own structures to improve combat efficiency in light of the threat posed by nuclear war. For example, in 1955, the army had replaced the Army Field Forces with the Continental Army Command, so that there would be fewer commands reporting directly to the chief of staff. The Continental Army Command was responsible for the Military District of Washington and the six armies in the United States. Other tasks allocated to Continental Army Command were training active and reserve formations, forward planning of the army's development and weapons, and planning the ground defense of the continental United States.

The "Pentomic" Division

The need for the army to take into account the demands of nuclear as well as conventional warfare demanded a radical restructuring of the basic division. The assumptions about nuclear warfare suggested that there might not be a solid front of the type for which the 17,000-man infantry division had been organized, so this triangular formation of three regiments supported by specialist units was revised in 1956. The new so-called "pentomic" arrangement of five self-contained battle groups in a 13,500-man division supported by artillery units deploying guns and missiles capable of carrying nuclear or conventional warheads. The armored division needed less modification as it was already structured for a more self-contained role on a fluid battlefield. All active divisions had been converted to the new structure by 1960 and the reserve and national guard divisions by 1961.

The seven divisions located in the United States were the nation's strategic reserve. On May 20, 1958, four of the divisions (two infantry and two airborne) became the Strategic Army Corps and were maintained at a high state of readiness for rapid deployment in the event of any emergency. The other three divisions were the Strategic Army Corps reserve, the base on which the army would be expanded in the event of prolonged hostilities.

Throughout the late 1950s, these and other organizational changes were complemented by the development and introduction of more modern weapons and an improved army aviation arm.

There were other major developments in this period. On January 31, 1958, the United States launched its first satellite, Explorer I. It was developed by the army, but after several successful launches, the Army Ballistic Missile Agency was transferred to NASA (National Aeronautics and Space Administration) on October 21, 1959, and the army thus ended its involvement in space matters. For the air defense of North America, the United States and Canada on May 19, 1958, created the North American Air Defense Command with headquarters in Colorado Springs, Colorado. On December 30, 1959, the U.S.S. *George Washington* was commissioned as the world's first operational submarine with a primary armament of nuclear-tipped ballistic missiles, in this instance 16 submarine-launched Polaris weapons; the submarine started its first combat patrol just under 11 months later.

Kennedy and a Revised American Policy

In January 1960, John F. Kennedy took over from Eisenhower as president. Under the new administration, another fundamental change in U.S. military affairs soon developed. The likelihood of a nuclear war had declined, while Soviet support for "wars of national liberation" had increased over the same period. It was also abundantly clear how angry Khrushchev was with the United States as a result of the "Powers incident," which occurred on May 7, 1960. A Lockheed U-2 high-altitude airplane on a reconnaissance flight of the U.S.S.R. was downed

Right: President John F. Kennedy inherited from Eisenhower the administration of a country facing the threat of rampant Soviet and communist expansion in many parts of the world.

Far Right: May 7, 1960, was a turning point in American-Soviet relations: on that day, a Lockheed U-2 "spyplane" piloted by Francis Gary Powers was downed by a surface-to-air missile near the Soviet city of Sverdlovsk during an illegal overflight of the U.S.S.R.

by a Soviet missile near Sverdlovsk. The pilot, Francis Gary Powers, escaped from his crashing machine and was captured by the Soviets and imprisoned after a high-publicity trial.

Despite the poor outlook and tense Soviet-American relations, Kennedy was determined to search for peace. The president stated in his budget speech of March 1961 that the United States would undertake "efforts to explore all possibilities and to take every step to lessen tensions, to attain peaceful solutions, and to secure arms limitation." Kennedy was firmly of the opinion that diplomacy and defense were complementary to each other, and not alternatives. The president had his feet firmly rooted in reality, however, and knew that the search for peace would be long. Kennedy decided that U.S. military capabilities should be more flexible than they had been and therefore better able to match the defense requirements of an evolving national strategy. Kennedy wanted a military establishment that was strong enough to survive and retaliate in the event of a general war, yet responsive enough to tackle and defeat any communist effort to erode the size and will of the free world in a limited war. Kennedy put it to Congress: "Any potential aggressor contemplating an attack on any part of the free world with any kind of weapons, conventional or nuclear, must know that our response will be suitable, selective, swift, and effective."

The Doctrine of Flexible Response

This opened an era in which flexible response replaced the idea of massive retaliation. The change came none too soon; massive retaliation was an obsolete concept, and flexible response opened the possibility of countermeasures and counteractions tailored to the specific situation. The inevitable result was another restructuring of the forces, together with their administrative organization and command apparatus, to make them both more flexible and more cost-effective. An immediate consequence was the revival of the army, which had languished in the Eisenhower years, but was now rightly seen as one of the major tools for the doctrine of flexible response.

Kennedy's chosen implement was a new secretary of defense, Robert S. McNamara, who inherited the first stages of the 1958 reorganization of the defense establishment and greatly accelerated it. Kennedy's instructions gave McNamara two main tasks: the development of the services with a structure suitable to implement flexible response, without considering predetermined or arbitrary financial limitations, and the operation of the restructured services at the lowest possible cost.

Centralized Planning and Control

McNamara was a keen advocate of centralized planning and control, and

Robert S. McNamara
For further references see pages
18, 19, 20, 22, 39, 57, 68, 90, 103, 126

The most important twin-rotor helicopter used by the U.S. Army in Vietnam was the Boeing Vertol CH-47 Chinook, which was designed to carry 40 fully equipped troops or an equivalent weight of freight transported either internally or as a slung load. This is an example of the CH-47A, the initial production model, which was powered by two 2,650-shaft horsepower Lycoming T55-L-7 turboshafts driving a pair of three-blade rotors, each 60 feet in diameter. The fuselage was 51 feet long, and access to the rectangular-section hold was provided by a hydraulically operated rear ramp/door. The type had a maximum speed of 190 miles an hour at sea level, and at a maximum take-off weight of 46,000 pounds, it could carry 44 troops, or 24 stretchers plus attendants, or 16,000 pounds of freight.

with the support of the Joint Chiefs of Staff, he now set about the difficult task of determining the plans and forces necessary to implement these revised national security policies. The forces themselves were divided by roles such as strategic retaliation, general purpose, and reserve. Only if these forces conformed to McNamara's "program package" concept (mission capability balanced in relation to cost-effectiveness) were they recommended for funding.

In its early stages, the Kennedy administration had three primary defense objectives: strengthening the United States' retaliatory nuclear forces, increasing of conventional forces so that an effective yet flexible response could be made to limited challenges, and improving the overall effectiveness and efficiency of the defense establishment.

The first objective was achieved by the installation of intercontinental ballistic missiles (ICBM) in sites "hardened" for protection against nuclear attack, and by increasing the number of nuclear-powered submarines carrying the Polaris submarine-launched missile.

The second objective was achieved by an increase in the size of the services: the air force and navy were allowed comparatively small gains, but the army swelled from 860,000 to 1,060,000 by the end of 1961. This increase resulted in part from calling several National Guard formations into federal service as a result of the crisis that resulted in the building of the Berlin Wall, but even after these formations were demobbed in 1962, the army retained a strength of 970,000 men and was allowed to activate two more divisions for a first-line strength of 16 divisions. The additional strength also allowed the army to fill the

ranks of under-strength units, and an increase in annual appropriations from $10.1 to $12.4 billion allowed important materiel acquisitions such as new vehicles, aircraft, missiles, and other equipment.

The third objective was achieved by organizational and procedural changes using the latest management and computer techniques. The Office of the Secretary of Defense centralized under its own control many functions previously administered by the individual services. McNamara made a great effort to standardize items used throughout the services by the creation of the Defense Supply Agency. This achieved some notable successes, but there were also some striking and extremely costly failures, such as the naval version of the General Dynamics F-111 tactical fighter.

Two other important developments of 1961 were the creation of the Defense Intelligence Agency and Strike Command. The Defense Intelligence Agency was designed to coordinate all defense-related intelligence operations at a high level so that the secretary of defense received one integrated report instead of three individual service intelligence assessments. Strike Command was intended to provide the U.S. military establishment with an immediate-reaction combination of ground and air-support forces. The structure combined the assets of the Strategic Army Corps and the air force's Tactical Air Command, which retained control of these elements until an emergency was declared and Strike Command was brought into play.

Revision of the Army

The effects of the review undertaken by the secretary of defense's staff in 1961 and approved by the president in 1962 under the terms of the Reorganization Act of 1958 were felt most strongly by the Department of the Army's staff and by the technical services.

The army staff had the main responsibility for determining policy and the appropriate plans, while decisions were implemented by the field commands. Most of the technical services were abolished, for it was McNamara's intention to revise army organization into a more functional structure with centralized research and development, personnel, training, and supply elements. Positions such as Chief Chemical Officer, Chief of Ordnance, and Quartermaster General were removed entirely, and the Chief Signal Officer and Chief of Transportation became special staff officers rather than heads of services. The Chief of Engineers retained his status only with regard to civil functions undertaken by the corps; his military functions were subordinated to the Deputy Chief of Staff for Logistics. Of the technical services, only the office of Surgeon General survived.

Among the administrative services, the Adjutant General and the Chief of Finance lost their statutory status and, like the Chief Signal Officer and Chief of Transportation, became special staff of-ficers. At the same level, an Office of Personnel Operations was created to supervise all assignments and career development. Many of the most important functions of the Quartermaster General were reallocated to the new Defense Supply Agency, but the Quartermaster General retained responsibility for tasks such as graves registration, laundry facilities, and commissaries.

Most of the responsibilities lost by the army staff and the technical services were given to Continental Army Command and two new organizations, Army Materiel Command and Army Combat Developments Command. Continental Army Command had responsibility for almost all of the army schools and for the training of individuals and units within the continental United States. It lost to the Army Materiel Command the responsibility for testing and evaluation, and to the Army Combat Developments Command the responsibility for all combat developments.

Army Materiel Command assumed many of the tasks previously handled by the technical services, establishing

The ZU-23-2 was one of the most effective light antiaircraft weapons fielded by the communist forces in the Vietnam War, and its capabilities placed distinct limitations on the type of attack that could be mounted by low-level aircraft. The whole equipment was towed by a light truck and based on a triangular platform with two wheels and a tow bar. In firing position the wheels were collapsed and the platform made stable by three screw jacks.

Corporal, 1st Brigade, 101st Airborne Division, U.S. Army, South Vietnam, 1965.

This non-commissioned officer is seen with the type of dress and kit worn in Operation "Highland." The division was completely outfitted with the 1963 pattern of jungle fatigues later in the year, but during this period, the men wore the OG107 fatigue uniform. This man wears his uniform over a white T shirt, and carries an M14 rifle with other equipment supported by the M1956 webbing.

subcommands to deal with them. In overall terms, it took responsibility for research, development, testing, production, procurement, storage, maintenance, and distribution of materiel of all types.

Army Combat Developments Command undertook the development of doctrines of an organizational and operational nature, the creation of materiel objectives and qualitative requirements, field experiments and war games, and cost-effectiveness assessments. In short, the task of the Army Combat Developments Command was to decide how the army should be organized and equipped, and how it was to fight.

The Reorganization Objective Army Division

This wholesale reorganization of the army's higher and specialist echelons was accompanied by a wide-ranging revision of the army's tactical structure to make it more responsive to the doctrine of flexible response. The pentomic division, which experience had proved to be deficient in manpower and in staying power for sustained operations was eliminated. The new type of division, organized to provide a balance between firepower and mobility, was known as the ROAD (Reorganization Objective Army Division). From 1962, four types of division (airborne, armored, infantry, and mechanized) were created with a common base and three brigade headquarters. The common base included a headquarters company, a military police company, a reconnaissance squadron, four artillery battalions, and single battalions of engineer, signal, medical, supply and transportation, and maintenance troops. The four types of division differed in the blend of the three combat brigades, for the actual numbers and types of component battalions could be modified to suit the operational needs of the specific theater. The infantry division typically controlled eight infantry and two tank battalions, but could have as many as 15 battalions under command.

The first such formations were the recently reactivated 1st Armored and 5th Infantry (Mechanized) Divisions, which were used for a thorough and very successful evaluation of the ROAD concept during 1962. The army therefore began to convert its other 14 divisions along the same lines during 1963, and the reserve and national guard divisions followed in a program that was completed in 1964.

Enhanced Battlefield Mobility

The army also wanted to improve the battlefield mobility of its divisions, and in 1962, it undertook a major comparison of land and air vehicles in terms of efficiency and cost. As a result, the army recommended the creation of air combat and transport units with helicopters that could carry men plus an armament of rockets and/or machine guns. This raised the question of whether or not the army was seeking to encroach on an air force mission, but McNamara decided that the result could be so important that a major trial was warranted. The 11th Air Assault Division was organized in February 1963 and undertook a two-year evaluation of the air assault concept. This study showed that the concept of air mobility had distinct advantages, and in 1965 it was decided to test the concept under operational conditions in Vietnam.

The 11th Air Assault Division was deactivated and transformed at Fort Benning, Georgia, into the air-mobile 1st Cavalry Division. (The 2nd Infantry Division took over the men and equipment left by the 1st Cavalry Division in South Korea.) The new 1st Cavalry Division had 15,785 men and 1,600 vehicles (only half the number of the standard division), but it possessed 428 helicopters. The division was equipped with the same number of rifles and automatic weapons as the standard division, but had lighter support weapons in the form of 105-mm (4.13-inch) howitzers that could be moved by helicopter and an aerial rocket artillery battalion in place of the standard division's general support artillery battalion. As the division was designed for complete air-mobility, its equipment weighed only 10,000 tons, less than one-third of the figure for the standard division's equipment.

Trouble Spots in Asia

The preoccupation of the defense establishment with nuclear warfare in the Eisenhower administrations had an adverse effect on developments in other areas. The United States had made a deliberate decision then not to become embroiled in limited wars. Events soon showed, however, that international problems occurred and had to be met by non-nuclear means. On some occasions, this meant military and economic aid; on others, the despatch of conventional forces.

In these circumstances, it was a clear advantage to strengthen the capabilities of friendly and even neutral nations that would otherwise possibly call for American aid. Thus the United States continued the Military Assistance Program started by President Harry S. Truman before the Korean War, supplying many Middle Eastern, Asian, and European countries with military aid, adviser groups, and military missions. This added considerably to U.S. military expenditure at a time when strenuous

efforts were being made to save money, but it was thought well worth the cost for political as well as military reasons.

In Korea, the United States kept two divisions in positions south of the demilitarized zone created by the Panmunjom armistice and also supplied the South Korean army with considerable aid. The communists broke the truce many occasions during the 1950s, but the presence of two high-grade American divisions in strong defensive positions helped to prevent these events from flaring into full-scale hostilities.

In general, however, the area farther south created the greatest problems for the United States in the period after the Korean War. The two major trouble spots were the large island of Formosa and, still farther south, Indochina.

Communist Versus Nationalist China

Formosa had reverted to its traditional Chinese name of Taiwan after the surrender of its Japanese garrison in 1945

During the 1950s, the U.S. Marine Corps made great strides in the refinement of its assault capability. One of the most important developments was the adoption of the helicopter as a primary assault vehicle. This is an early type, the Sikorsky HUS-1 Seahorse, which could carry 12 troops with a single 1,525-horsepower piston engine.

and had been held since 1949 as the bastion of Generalissimo Chiang Kai-shek's Kuomintang (or nationalist) party after its defeat in the Chinese Civil War by the communists under Mao Tse-tung. With the support of the United States, the Kuomintang government continued to assert that it was the rightful government of all China. The Kuomintang also held the Quemoy, Matsu, Nanchi, and Tachen groups of small islands immediately off the coast of mainland China, though the Nanchi and Tachen groups were captured by the communists on January 18, 1955. The Quemoy and Matsu groups provided an effective buffer to any possible communist efforts against Taiwan. On July 24, 1950, Quemoy came under intense communist artillery bombardment, and the threat of such communist efforts was one of the main reasons for the establishment of a U.S. military assistance group for Taiwan on January 30, 1951. During this period, the 7th Fleet included as part of its responsibilities the prevention of movement between the mainland and Taiwan in either direction. On February 2, 1953, President Eisenhower removed this obligation from the 7th Fleet, though a resurgence of the communist threat in mid-1954 led the president to declare, on August 17, that any communist move against Formosa would be opposed by the 7th Fleet.

On September 3, 1954, a renewed bombardment of Quemoy indicated that the communists might be planning a move against Taiwan, and the 7th Fleet was moved into the area. On December 2 of the same year, the United States and the Chinese nationalists signed a mutual defense treaty that effectively provided American recognition of "Formosa and the Pescadores" as a Chinese nationalist country. The bombardment of Quemoy and Matsu continued, and in January 1955 the Nanchi and Tachen Islands were threatened. On January 24, Eisenhower asked Congress for emergency powers to use U.S. forces to protect Taiwan if necessary. The 7th Fleet helped to evacuate 17,000 civilians, as well as 25,000 military personnel, between February 6 and 11. On June 7, 1955, an uneasy truce settled over the inshore islands.

Events flared once more on August 23, 1958, when communist artillery started to blockade Quemoy with a continuous bombardment that cut both civil and military supply lines. The 7th Fleet convoyed supplies by sea and air, and the communist effort tailed away in October before finally ending in June 1959. Several similar incidents occurred before 1969, when the United States withdrew its commitment to the area as relations with China improved under the administration of President Richard M. Nixon.

Disaster in Indochina

The web of American relations with Indochina was more tangled and ultimately tragic. Before World War II, the French colony of Indochina consisted of the five regions of Tonkin, Annam, Cochin-China, Laos, and Cambodia. Resistance to French rule began to develop during the 1930s from both nationalist and communist groups. Although it was small, the opposition was well established by the outbreak of World War II in 1939.

When France fell to Germany in June 1940, the isolated French outpost of Indochina could offer no real resistance to Japanese encroachment and in 1941 was occupied. In this year, a communist leader, Nguyen Ai Qoc (later known as Ho Chi Minh, or the enlightened one)

Ho Chi Minh
For further references
see pages
25, 27

The key figure in the creation of the Vietnamese communist party was Ho Chi Minh, seen here during a meeting with General Philippe Leclerc, the first French commander in Indochina after World War II. At this stage, the relations between the two men were relatively cordial, the bitter war between the communists and the French had not yet flared up.

established the Vietnam Doc Lap Dong Minh Ho (League for the Independence of Vietnam), later known as the Viet Minh. During World War II, the communist guerrillas of the Viet Minh received Kuomintang and American assistance in their fight, under the military leadership of Vo Nguyen Giap, against the Japanese. By August 1945, the Viet Minh controlled much of the jungle region of northern Vietnam, and in the power vacuum left by the surrender of the Japanese, Ho Chi Minh declared the Democratic Republic of Vietnam at Hanoi on September 2, 1945.

In the northern part of Vietnam, the Kuomintang forces took the surrender of the Japanese forces and either sold or bartered most of their weapons to the Viet Minh. South of the 16th parallel, British-commanded Indian troops began to arrive on September 12 and had to use surrendered Japanese troops to restore order. The first French troops arrived on October of the same year and started to regain control of southern Vietnam. By the end of 1945, the French had regained control of southern Vietnam, but in the north the Viet Minh civil and military administration still ruled. On March 6, 1946, France recognized the independence of Vietnam within the new Indochinese Federation and the French Union. The same day, French troops landed at Haiphong, northern Vietnam's main port, to begin the reconquest of the area held by the Viet Minh.

France managed to regain most of the country in a campaign of considerable savagery on both sides, but in January 1950 the U.S.S.R. and communist China recognized the Viet Minh. This paved the way for the delivery of Soviet weapons to the Viet Minh and for the training of their forces in southern China. From then on the task of the French became increasingly difficult, and France asked the United States for help against the communists. The United States was willing to supply economic aid, military equipment, and supplies, but was unwilling to commit U.S. troops or aircraft. After a series of major setbacks in October 1950, the French lost much of northern Vietnam, only to regain it under a new commander who arrived in December 1950. The period between 1951 and 1953 was characterized by bitter guerrilla warfare that left the French in command of the garrisoned cities and towns, and the Viet Minh in control of the rest of the country.

The gradually worsening French position prompted a surge of American aid between March and September 1953, but a major Viet Minh effort between October 1953 and April 1954 effectively sealed the end of French rule. The final act of this initial tragedy was the siege of Dien Bien Phu, where, between November 20, 1953 and May 7, 1954, a force of some 15,000 French and local troops were defeated by Giap's men. For the loss of 25,000 of their own number, the Viet Minh divisions killed 5,000 of the French garrison and captured 10,000 more, half of them wounded. Only 73 of the French garrison escaped.

The Geneva Accords

Exhausted by the war and shattered by the defeat at Dien Bien Phu, the French came to the Geneva Conference on Far Eastern Affairs (April 26 to July 21, 1954) and conceded defeat. The conference resulted in the Geneva Accords, comprising a signed ceasefire and an unsigned final declaration. As far as Vietnam was concerned, the Geneva Accords ordered a military disengagement and the creation of a temporary demilitarized zone across the narrow waist of the country on the 17th parallel. The areas north and south

Ho Chi Minh, the *nomme de guerre* selected by Nguyen Ai Quoc, meaning ''he who enlightens.''

Viet Cong
For further references see pages 26, 27, 28, 29, 30, 31, 33, 34, 35, 36, 39, 41, 44, 47, 48, 49, 51, 54, 65, 67, 69, 70, *76*, 78, 79, 83, 92, 93, 100, *103*, 110, 129, 131

A member of South Vietnam's militia organization receives advice from a professional soldier during camouflage training.

Laos
For further references see pages 28, 32, 34, 41, 45, 46, 56, 59, 70, 76, 78, 85, 101, 126

Cambodia
For further references see pages 28, 70, 85, 93, 94, 113, 116, 126, 129, 131

of this line were to be run by the Viet Minh and the French respectively. The demilitarized zone was 6.2 miles (10 km) wide, and no forces from either side were to enter it. Civilians were free to choose between the two zones, and general elections were to be organized two years later to reunite the country according to the "national will of the Vietnamese people." Separate parts of the Geneva Accords recognized Cambodia and Laos, which had declared themselves independent in November 1953 and July 1949 respectively, as independent neutral states. France soon started to withdraw her armed forces from Indochina, but continued to provide training for the forces of Cambodia, Laos, and South Vietnam.

The administrations of both the northern and southern zones of Vietnam refused to accept the division of Vietnam, and the administration of premier Ngo Dinh Diem in the south also refused to accept the validity of any future election on the grounds that free elections would be impossible in the northern zone. The United States accepted the Geneva Accords, but refused to become a signatory, instead reserving the right to take whatever action it thought necessary if the terms of the agreement were breached. However, the United States assumed the burden of supplying military equipment and training as well as economic aid to South Vietnam after the departure of the French. On January 20, 1955, South Vietnam agreed that its army would be reorganized by the Americans and the French on the basis of 100,000 active troops and 150,000 reserves. The overall program was controlled by a French officer, General Paul Ely, and under his supervision was an American training mission.

As the armistice came into effect and created what was in effect two separate countries, North Vietnam and South Vietnam, some 800,000 people from the north moved into the south, while the flow in the other direction was about 100,000 people. Many of the latter were Viet Minh activists. At the direct instruction of Ho Chi Minh, however, vital Viet Minh cadres remained in the south as a nucleus for further action. The communists also retained control of several base areas (or secret zones) in the south.

The Geneva Conference helped to crystallize thinking in the United States about the spread of communism in Southeast Asia. As a result, the U.S. became the chief sponsor of the Southeast Asia Treaty, which was signed in Manila on September 8, 1954. The other signatories were Australia, France, New Zealand, Pakistan, the Philippines, Thailand, and the United Kingdom. The purposes of the treaty were to provide collective defense and economic co-operation in Southeast Asia, and the protection of the region's weaker countries against aggression. The treaty was patterned after the North Atlantic Treaty in its basic objectives and

structure, and on February 19, 1955, the Southeast Asia Treaty Organization came into effective existence.

A Changed American Rationale

When the first American aid reached the French in Indochina in 1950, it represented only a small part of the complete Military Assistance Program. At this stage, American involvement was limited to supporting an ally that was seeking to defeat a nationalist movement which, with Chinese and Soviet encouragement, had established links with the communist bloc. The United States hoped at this stage that France would regain control of Vietnam, realize that self-determination was the best course, and give Vietnam its independencies. The Viet Minh victory overtook both French and American ambitions in the region, and the continued support of the United States for South Vietnam altered in rationale as well as

A relatively narrow country, South Vietnam had a long coastline and extensive inland waterways. Both provided the Viet Cong with good access routes and needed extensive patroling to keep them from becoming highways – rather than merely being paths – for communist infiltration.

extent. American support was now supplied not to a colonial power, but to a small country striving for survival in the face of communist aggression. The issue was complicated by the existence of smaller but less well-organized communist efforts in Cambodia and Laos, and by the ideological split between China and the U.S.S.R. after 1957. The United States therefore feared that the "war of national liberation" in Vietnam was another test of resolve between the communist and free worlds, and might intensify into a global confrontation between the two superpowers.

In the years after the French defeat, therefore, the level of U.S. aid developed in quantity and complexity. In fact, it began to overshadow other elements of the country's international program and became a serious test of U.S. determination to see the matter to a conclusion.

The war between the French and the Viet Minh was essentially a ground war. U.S. involvement consisted of a small number of personnel, mainly from the army, to supervise the financial and military aid being supplied to the French and the forces of the French-sponsored administration of Emperor Bao Dai. This situation continued up to the time of France's defeat, when there were about 400 American service personnel in Vietnam, most of them in Saigon, the capital of what was to become South Vietnam. These advisers remained in Vietnam and began the major task of creating a South Vietnamese army based on the 200,000-man force that had fought with the French.

Problems for South Vietnam

One of the first obstacles faced by the new government in South Vietnam was the taint of its connection with the French colonial administration. Another difficulty was persuading the people of South Vietnam that American aid not mean that the United States had its own colonial ambitions in Southeast Asia. Other problems included a predominance of Roman Catholics in the government of a mainly Buddhist country, the continued political influence of two religious sects

(the Cao Dai and the Hoa Hao) even after the government had taken control of their previously autonomous military forces, the continued resistance of the Montagnards of the central highlands to any type of central authority, and the near chaos of a largely rural society which had lost the industries and mineral resources of the north. These factors gave the communists the ability to control a large part of the country unhindered by the activities of a generally corrupt civil administration.

Diem ruled autocratically rather than democratically, but did manage to restore some order to the country and get the economy back on track once more. There was considerable resentment about the emperor, who by moving abroad had effectively deserted the country. Late in 1955, Diem deposed the emperor, submitted the matter to a referendum, and on October 26, 1955, declared the Republic of Vietnam with himself as president. Further progress resulted from Diem's continued strong rule: the outmaneuvering of dissident army officers about to stage a coup, the crushing of a strong group of Saigon gangsters (the Binh Xuyen), the resettlement of refugees from the north, and the initiation of a land reform program.

Ngo Dinh Diem
For further references see pages
26, *28*, 29, 30, 31, 36, 38, 39, 95

Saigon
For further references see pages
30, 32, 40, 41, 44, 47, 60, 67, 68, 93, 95, 110, 121, 127, 130, 131

Ngo Dinh Diem was President of South Vietnam in 1955. He was overthrown by the military in 1963.

Shortly before the planned date for the national elections in early 1956, the French pulled their last forces out of Vietnam. Once again, Diem objected to the idea of the national elections. Diem's objections were supported by the United States, which said that "there must first be conditions which preclude intimidation or coercion of the electorate."

Communist Plans for South Vietnam

Between the Geneva Accords and the spring of 1956, the communists had kept a low profile. In South Vietnam, Viet Minh cadres were quietly awaiting the elections that were expected to record a landslide victory for the communists, who now controlled the electoral process in the more highly populated north and could expect to get a percentage of the vote in the south. In North Vietnam, the communists were asserting their authority over the country after destroying a popular revolt and undertaking a reign of terror to bring the rural areas under central control. The South Vietnamese government's refusal to hold elections was therefore a blow, for it removed the communists' chance to gain overall control by peaceful, "democratic" means.

With easy victory forestalled, the communists ordered the Viet Minh in the south to resume their insurgency campaign, against the South Vietnamese instead of the French. This took time, for the cadres in the south had to be revitalized, resupplied, reorganized, and reinforced. It now became common in South Vietnam to call the Viet Minh insurgents the Viet Cong, a dismissive contraction of the local term for Vietnamese communists. Like all guerrilla forces, the Viet Cong sought to improve their chances of survival by relying as little as possible on external sources of supply. In South Vietnam, they used a mixture of coercion and propaganda to swell their numbers and get supplies. As the Viet Cong geared themselves for action, their North Vietnamese masters made a conscious decision to bring down the government of South Vietnam by force. From 1958, political cadres and military reinforce-

ments began to flow south from North Vietnam.

Outbreak of the Terror Campaign

The initial weapon in this campaign was terror. The Viet Cong launched a program of assassination, kidnapping, sabotage, and attacks on the South Vietnamese civil guard and local defense units. Late in 1960, the North Vietnamese sponsored a National Front for the Liberation of South Vietnam as an organization that would attract nationalists as well as communists.

Despite the fact that they had fought a protracted counterinsurgency war in the country, the French had trained the units of what was now the Army of the Republic of Vietnam (A.R.V.N., pronounced "Arvin") on purely conventional lines. This made the A.R.V.N. only poorly able to tackle the problem of growing Viet Cong insurgency. French and American advisers made great efforts to develop the right skills in the South Vietnamese forces, but were hampered by their own lack of numbers, lack of internal and external resources, and lack of the right type of raw material on which to work. When the French pulled out of the country, another 350

Assassination and murder were two of the favorite weapons of the Viet Cong, and the threat was a powerful incentive for many South Vietnamese to provide the communists with the support they needed. This group of South Vietnamese was chained and murdered by the Viet Cong.

> **A.R.V.N.**
> For further references
> see pages
> 30, 32, 34, 36, 38, 39, 41,
> 51, 52, 54, 56, 60, 65, 67,
> 69, 70, 78, 79, 84, 93, 94,
> 95, 101, 124, 129, 131

Americans bolstered the effort of the existing 400-man group, but this reinforcement was used mainly to recover and repair American-supplied equipment rather than improve the training of the A.R.V.N. During 1956, the adviser and equipment roles were combined under the auspices of the Military Assistance Advisory Group, Vietnam.

Logistic Improvements

The advisers were based mainly in Saigon, where they helped the A.R.V.N. in high-level planning, logistics, and training. In 1960, however, the deteriorating situation in South Vietnam persuaded Diem to allow U.S. advisers into the field in an effort to improve the A.R.V.N.'s combat capability. Even so, American advisers were attached to A.R.V.N. units only down to battalion level, and the shortage of advisers meant that all field assignments were temporary and fairly arbitrary in location.

The growth of the Viet Cong insurgency coincided, most fortunately for the communist cause, with a increasing separation between Diem and the majority of the South Vietnamese people. Diem was increasingly separated from reality inside a coterie of relatives whom he had appointed to high positions, and the growing aloofness of Diem's family circle was a major factor in alienating the South Vietnamese people from the government. Diem continued to rule with complete autocracy, but several factors increasingly incensed the South Vietnamese people: the government's failure to involve ordinary people even at the local level of government, incredibly slow progress in the matter of land reform, the constant use of oppressive policing methods, and the arbitrary selection of policies in both civil and military matters. When Diem was pressed, he sought to pass off these failures as the inevitable consequences of fighting the communist menace which would be corrected as soon as a situation of national security and stability

The marines operated in the hot and very humid northern coastal region of South Vietnam, where thick vegetation was part of the natural cover that made ambushes easy.

had been reestablished. Diem's protestations were seen for the evasions they were and served only to alienate the South Vietnamese even further from the government. On November 4, 1960, there was a military revolt against Diem, but it was soon suppressed. Diem did not see the dangers inherent in this situation and continued as before.

Assassination and Kidnapping

During 1961, the Viet Cong stepped up their program of assassination and kidnapping. The program was directed mainly at members of the civil administration, especially at a local level, in order to speed up the disintegration of South Vietnam. Members of their families and important figures in civilian life at every level of South Vietnamese society also became targets. The Viet Cong program was very successful, and during 1961 the South Vietnamese people concluded with increasing correctness that their government was totally incapable of protecting them against the ravages of the

Viet Cong. By the fall of 1961, the Viet Cong had gained enough power in many parts of South Vietnam to threaten the continued viability of Diem's government.

President Kennedy sent missions to examine the situation in South Vietnam, and their reports and recommendations made alarming reading. Worried by the poor prospects of South Vietnam's survival, especially as the Viet Cong and North Vietnamese infiltrators had already done considerable damage to the fabric of the Geneva Accords, Kennedy decided in October 1961 that stronger measures from the United States were needed. On October 11, American military assistance was pledged to South Vietnam for the defeat of the Viet Cong menace. General Maxwell D. Taylor was sent to South Vietnam to investigate the most effective way in which U.S. support could be used. On October 26, Kennedy sent a personal message assuring Diem that he would continue to enjoy American support.

Kennedy had decided on a considerable increase in the U.S. commitment to South Vietnam, though he

Viet Cong prisoners are brought aboard a South Vietnamese coastal craft for interrogation during Operation "Market Time," a joint American and South Vietnamese undertaking, begun in the spring of 1965 and designed to check communist infiltration through coastal waters.

stopped short of deploying of troops in a combat role. During 1962, therefore, the numbers of U.S. advisers in South Vietnam increased to more than 11,000, about two-thirds of them from the U.S. Army. These men reported to the U.S. Military Assistance Command, Vietnam, set up in Saigon in February 1962 under General Paul D. Harkins. This new formation was a unified field command under the overall control of the Commander-in-Chief, Pacific, in turn responsible to the president via the Joint Chiefs of Staff and the secretary of defense.

An Expanded Adviser Force

This increase in U.S. personnel in South Vietnam more than tripled the numbers of men available as advisers which meant that for the first time advisers could be attached

to virtually all A.R.V.N. field units. Another modification to previous American support was the introduction of teams from the U.S. Army Special Forces to train Civilian Irregular Defense Groups among the South Vietnamese civil population in general, and the Montagnard tribesmen of the central highlands in particular.

The communist threat to the highlands had been growing more rapidly than elsewhere in South Vietnam, for just over the border in Laos, there was a strong communist party that enjoyed considerable support from the North Vietnamese. In the portion of eastern Laos bordering the western parts of North Vietnam and South Vietnam, the communists had established loose overall control over the frontier region. Here, the North Vietnamese created a network of small roads and trails that allowed men and equipment to be infiltrated from North Vietnam into South Viet-

The M551 Sheridan light tank was designed in 1959 to answer a need for an Armored Reconnaissance Airborne Assault Vehicle that would replace both the M41 light tank and the M56 90-mm (3·54-inch) tank destroyer. The vehicle was a conventional light tank with an unconventional weapon – a 152-mm (6-inch) barrel that could fire either the Shillelagh antitank missile, or "conventional" ammunition using a combustible cartridge case. The first prototype ran in 1962.

nam around the western end of the Demilitarized Zone along the 17th parallel. This network was collectively known as the Ho Chi Minh Trail; and although its component roads and trails were individually small, in total the Trail was a major route. It allowed the dispersed movement of large numbers of men and eventually a sizable quantity of the light materiel needed by the Viet Cong units, which at this stage of the war operated only as guerrilla forces. The Ho Chi Minh Trail, with its relay stations and logistical bases, was planned from the outset to support a sustained effort in South Vietnam. The Ho Chi Minh Trail itself ended at the South Vietnamese frontier, but in fact it continued into South Vietnam as an even more diffuse series of little trails impossible to distinguish from ordinary rural tracks.

The Concept of "Strategic Hamlets"

The Civilian Irregular Defense Groups manned the fortified outposts, or "strategic hamlets," located tactically close to the frontier and the trails coming over it. Advised by soldiers of the Special Forces, the men of the Civilian Irregular Defense Groups patrolled from their outposts in an effort to stop the flow of men and equipment entering South Vietnam from Laos, and so prevent or at least make it more difficult for the communists to control the central highlands.

During 1962, there was a worldwide effort to stabilize the position in Southeast Asia. On July 23, 1962, the Geneva Agreement on Laos was signed by 14 interested parties, who guaranteed the

The CCB (command and control boat), an important part of the U.S. riverine effort in South Vietnam, was in essence a Monitor Mk V with its 81-mm (3·2-inch) mortar well covered over to accommodate a command and communications facilities module. The rig at the stern was used to tow disabled craft.

independence and neutrality of Laos. South Vietnam and the United States hoped that this would help to stem the flow of North Vietnamese support for the Viet Cong through Laos, but the communists managed to retain control of the frontier region, and the flow of men and equipment continued unhindered. Even so, the 60,000 men trained by the Special Forces in 1962 and 1963 played a decisive part in preventing this steady flow from becoming a torrent, and as a result the communists failed to gain control of the central highlands and other parts of the South Vietnamese frontier region.

The task faced by the Special Forces and other advisers was difficult. They were faced with the problem of developing leadership qualities which the French had sought to discourage during the long years of their rule. The job was vital to the continued existence of South Vietnam, for this first wave of South Vietnamese leaders would have to spread the process to a succeeding wave of more junior leaders. It was a daunting proposition, for it meant that the U.S. advisers had to

come to terms with social, economic, and political views totally alien to their own so that they could communicate their ideas to South Vietnamese on the other side of a wide language and cultural gulf. The advisers also had to entrust their lives to foreign troops who were generally unproved in combat and often infiltrated by the enemy, all in the role where the Americans could only advise and not order.

This U.S. support for the A.R.V.N. and its civilian support elements helped to halt the deterioration of the situation in South Vietnam, but was inadequate to provide a solution. The Military Assistance Command, Vietnam, saw that a major non-combat contribution could be made by improving the A.R.V.N.'s support structure, and in 1962 the main weight of the American effort was devoted to operational support of the A.R.V.N. Particular emphasis was placed on improving the A.R.V.N.'s mobility, communications, logistics, and intelligence. In the short term, the greatest American contribution was made in the field of mobility;

The greatest tactical innovation of the Vietnam War was the use of the helicopter as a tactical transport, which gave the American forces a very high level of mobility in hostile terrain. The best known type used for this important task was the Bell UH-1 Iroquois, universally known as the "Huey" as its initial designation was HU-1. The main disadvantage of the UH-1 was its wide-chord main rotor with only two blades, which generated a very distinctive "slap-slap" sound that could be heard from some distance away.

the introduction of helicopters gave the A.R.V.N. far greater tactical mobility and helped it avoid ambushes on the vulnerable roads.

Arrival of American Helicopters

The first American helicopters reached South Vietnam on December 11, 1961, when two helicopter companies of the U.S. Army arrived with their Piasecki H-21 Shawnee twin-rotor machines of the type inevitably dubbed ''Flying Bananas'' because of the curvature of their fuselages. From 1963, the H-21 was replaced by the smaller but considerably faster and more versatile Bell UH-1 Iroquois, a turbine- rather than piston-engine type called the ''Huey.'' The ''Huey'' almost immediately became the symbol of the new type of war being waged in South Vietnam. Large numbers of helicopters allowed tactical mobility, making it possible for men and equipment to be collected from one point and transferred rapidly to another

in a campaign that therefore came to lack a defined front line.

Thus, the war in South Vietnam soon evolved into a series of apparently unconnected clashes on a kind of giant chessboard. Its squares lacked sharp boundaries, but covered geographical areas that varied from the under-populated but densely forested highlands through the extensively farmed and highly populated river valleys of the coastal plains, to the flooded rice paddies and swampy estuaries of the south where the River Mekong flows into the sea.

The Battle of Ap Bac

The nature of the problem in South Vietnam was highlighted in the Battle of Ap Bac, a small but significant affair that took place in the Mekong Delta's Plain of Reeds in January 1963. A Viet Cong radio station was reportedly operating from the village, which was thought to be garrisoned by only a company-sized Viet Cong force. The A.R.V.N. despatched a

Another major role for the "Huey" was casualty evacuation. The availability of helicopters in this role meant that wounded men could be rushed to first-class medical facilities without delay, which not only reduced the number of deaths resulting from battle wounds, but also boosted general morale among the fighting troops.

Another innovation in the battlefield use of helicopters was suppressive fire with machine guns and rockets. When rocket launchers were fitted they were generally aligned along the helicopter's line of flight and fired by the pilot at targets on the ground ahead of his machine. The machine guns were generally fitted in the cabin doorways on a trainable mounting that allowed the gunners to engage any and all targets they spotted in the landing zone.

multi-battalion force of infantry, ranger, helicopter, and armored units, together with 51 American advisers. The units ran into a more formidable opponent than anticipated: 400 regulars of the 514th Viet Cong Battalion. Within a few moments of the battle's beginning, five helicopters had been lost (one to mechanical failure and four to enemy fire), but the A.R.V.N. troops advanced very slowly, mindful of a standing order from Diem that casualties should not be suffered. As a result, it took one A.R.V.N. commander three and a half hours to advance his armored personnel carriers 1,500 yards (1,370 m) – 0·8 of a mile – against Viet Cong equipped solely with small arms whose bullets could no more than scratch the armor of the M113 carriers. The advisers suggested an airborne drop east of Ap Bac to cut the Viet Cong's line of retreat, but the troops landed west of the village, and when the advisers suggested a concentrated artillery barrage, it was delivered at the extraordinarily slow rate of just four rounds an hour. Then a South Vietnamese air attack hit a friendly unit, and finally the Viet Cong escaped under cover of darkness. The Battle of Ap Bac resulted in the loss of five American helicopters and damage to 11 more, together with the deaths of three U.S. advisers and at least 65 A.R.V.N. soldiers – without causing the 514th Viet Cong Battalion anything more than a little inconvenience.

So useful did the helicopter become that the initial allocation of one helicopter company to each of the A.R.V.N.'s four corps was soon modified to one helicopter company to each A.R.V.N. division. The success of helicopters in boosting the A.R.V.N.'s tactical mobility can be gauged from the fact that the North Vietnamese were soon sending light antiaircraft weapons south to the Viet Cong, which spurred the development of armed helicopters. At first, "Hueys" were fitted with machine guns in their doorways so that the gunner(s) could saturate any area thought to conceal Viet Cong weapons. This early expedient soon gave way to a mixture of fixed machine guns and rocket pods on the sides of the helicopter, and finally a dedicated gunship version

Left: Photographed from a sister helicopter, this troop-carrying armed helicopter is a UH-1D, the first production version of the Bell Model 205 design. The original UH-1A and its derivatives were of the Model 204 designed for carrying eight troops, and the Model 205 introduced a larger cabin for greater payload. This could include 12 troops, or six stretchers and one attendant, or 4,000 pounds of freight.

Below: This scene is typical of an air cavalry helicopter landing, with UH-1B helicopters arriving to deliver men and departing to make room for new arrivals.

U.S. and South
Vietnamese personnel
on a light craft armed
with a turret-mounted
20-mm cannon in the
bows.

of the "Huey" utility helicopter, the AH-1 Huey Cobra, with a slim fuselage and a two-man crew seated in tandem on vertically staggered seats, was created. The gunner occupied the front seat and controlled the turreted chin armament, generally an automatically loaded 40-mm grenade launcher and a 7.62-mm (0.3-inch) Minigun, whose externally powered rotating assembly of six barrels could spew out a huge volume of fire. The pilot occupied the rear seat and generally controlled the forward-firing armament of machine guns and/or pods for varying numbers of 2.75-inch (70-mm) unguided rockets that could be fired singly or in a rippled salvo.

An Improved Military Situation?

By the spring of 1963, the military situation in South Vietnam seemed to be improving, even though the United States

was becoming increasingly worried about the A.R.V.N.'s poor fighting skills and apparent reluctance to learn such skills. Close action was discouraged, as it caused casualties, and officers from the rank of major upward were unwilling to go into the field since combat was beneath their dignity. Yet, with the aid of American advisers, equipment, and technical support, the military situation was slowly becoming better.

Exactly the opposite was the case with the political situation, where the repression, corruption, and favoritism of the administration was continuing to alienate most of South Vietnam's civil population from Diem's regime. Continued pleas for reform were made by the American ambassador and other interested parties, but nothing was achieved. From May of the same year, the government seriously mishandled large-scale demonstrations by Buddhists in most parts of the country. As a result, the United States refused to hand over subsidies which had been offered for imports and the South Vietnamese special forces, which had been used for attacks on Buddhist temples.

The Death of Diem

The inevitable result of Diem's maladministration was another military revolt on November 1, 1963, by a group of senior military officers. Diem and his brother were killed, and Diem's government was overthrown. The United States recognized the incoming provisional administration headed by Nguyen Ngoc Tho, the former vice-president, but real power lay with the military junta headed by Major General Duong Van Minh. Eighteen months of political turmoil followed. On January 30, 1964, the government was overthrown by another military revolt, this time headed by Major General Nguyen Khanh. This coup led to slightly reduced internal tension within South Vietnam.

During this period, the American presence in South Vietnam had increased to just under 23,000 men, just under two-thirds of them provided by the U.S. Army. This allowed the Military Advisory Command, Vietnam, to increase the level of operational support it could offer to the A.R.V.N. and permitted it to create adviser teams to allocate to South Vietnamese provinces and districts as part of the rural pacification program. Even so, the political turmoil in South Vietnam was ideal soil for the growth of the Viet Cong's influence, and the Viet Cong burgeoned to a strength of about 100,000. About one-third were "main force" troops organized for combat in battalions and regiments; the other two-thirds were support troops who kept control of communist-dominated areas and supplied the "main force" units with reinforcements, weapons and ammunition, other equipment, and food. It was also notable that the increased communist strength in South Vietnam included useful numbers of North Vietnamese regular troops infiltrated into South Vietnam along the Ho Chi Minh Trail. In much of South Vietnam, therefore, the Viet Cong were

so dominant that they constituted a "government" effective enough to levy "taxes." The South Vietnamese forces could move through these areas without difficulty during daylight hours, but it was rightly estimated that "the night belongs to the VC." The threat of the Viet Cong meant that the people in the rural areas of the south could easily be bullied into support of the communist cause with food and shelter.

A considerable effort had also been made to relocate a large portion of the rural population into so-called "strategic hamlets", which were fortified villages designed to provide local residents with safe havens from the Viet Cong. Much had been hoped from the program, but by now it was clearly a failure and rapidly collapsed. At the same time, the Viet Cong felt their strength now warranted the extension of their campaign into the daylight hours. Daylight attacks multiplied in geographical extent and number. The A.R.V.N. casualty rate began to climb steeply, and even though American service personnel were still involved only as advisers, their losses also increased: in 1963, 42 U.S. Army personnel were killed; in 1964, this figure rose to 118.

The Death of President Kennedy

Three weeks after the killing of Diem, President Kennedy was assassinated and Vice President Lyndon B. Johnson was sworn in. He quickly became the inheritor of a steadily more precarious situation in South Vietnam. In March 1964, Secretary of Defense McNamara saw that the situation was deteriorating further under Khanh's rule, but also realized that the United States had little alternative but to continue its support of South Vietnam. Nothing else, he felt, could prevent the country from succumbing to communist aggression and so set off the "domino effect" which Western analysts thought would result in the fall of all the other Southeast Asian countries. Khanh consented to a program of national mobilization, and Johnson agreed to replace older A.R.V.N. equipment with new American materiel and to finance a 50,000-man expansion of the A.R.V.N.

Ho Chi Minh Trail
For further references
see pages
33, 45, 56, 76, 85, 101, 130

Nguyen Khanh
For further references
see pages
40, 43, 45, 46, 47, 49

Lyndon B. Johnson
For further references
see pages
40, 41, 43, 44, 45, 47, 48, 49, 51, 52, 56, 57, 60, 67, 68, 76, 90, 105, 124, 125, 127

The assassination of President Kennedy elevated Vice President Lyndon B. Johnson to the White House and saddled him with the increasing problems of the Southeast Asian situation.

At the same time, Johnson ordered the Joint Chiefs of Staff to plan retaliatory attacks on North Vietnam in the form of bombing raids that could be mounted at 72-hour notice. The president lacked any congressional mandate for such an operation and still hoped that South Vietnam would be able to survive with only limited U.S. support. But Johnson was a realist who saw the advantages of being prepared for more South Vietnamese failures.

In the middle of 1964, General Taylor became U.S. ambassador in Saigon, and General William C. Westmoreland succeeded General Harkins at the head of the Military Assistance Command, Vietnam. Shortly afterward, Khanh and the head of the South Vietnamese air force, Air Vice Marshal Nguyen Cao Ky, tried to embarrass the United States into greater support, including retaliatory air attacks on North Vietnam. They revealed that North Vietnamese soldiers were already operating in South Vietnam, and that the United States had in any case helped South Vietnam to send sabotage teams into North Vietnam for the last three years. Both assertions were true, but Taylor's investigation failed to find evidence that North Vietnamese units rather than individuals were fighting in South Vietnam.

William C. Westmoreland
For further references see pages
47, 50, 52, 54, 56, 57, 59, 60, 67, 68, 69, 70, 76, 78, 79, 84, 90, 92, 93, 94, 100, 101, 103, 105, 109, 110, 120, 122, 125, 126, 127, 128, 129, 131

The claim about sabotage teams was accurate, but was only part of the effort to destabilize North Vietnam through the infiltration of commando teams, the indoctrination of abducted North Vietnamese civilians who might then return home and sow dissent, and intelligence-gathering patrols off the North Vietnamese coast by destroyers of the 7th Fleet. Since May 1964, after the communists launched a major offensive in the Plain of Jars, armed reconnaissance flights had flown over Laos, with pilots ordered to retaliate if fired upon. These moves, designed to convince North Vietnam of the United States' real commitment to South Vietnam, were reinforced by the public admission that weapons and equipment were being stockpiled in South Vietnam in case it proved necessary to commit U.S. forces. The highest profile was therefore given to the dedication of the vast new air base at Da Nang.

Warnings to North Vietnam

These covert and semi-covert activities were complemented by overt warnings delivered to the North Vietnamese by Blair Seaborn, the Canadian member of the International Control Commission in Hanoi. None of these efforts worked, and the southward flow of North Vietnamese troops and materiel continued. By July 1964 the Viet Cong were strong enough to plant bombs in the streets of Saigon and harass Americans living in the South Vietnamese capital. This Viet Cong combination of military parity in the rural areas and a superiority of terror in the urban areas was instrumental in persuading an increasing number of U.S. intelligence officers that the communists were on the verge of a major offensive to crush the demoralized A.R.V.N. and overthrow South Vietnam's destabilized government.

In July 1964, several of President Johnson's advisers began to draft a congressional resolution authorizing American attacks on North Vietnam to check the supposedly imminent offensive. The president himself was more cautious, but then the North Viet-namese took matters into their own hands.

On August 22, 1964, the destroyer U.S.S. *Maddox* had completed an intelligence-gathering sweep along the coast of North Vietnam and was now steaming in the Gulf of Tonkin, well outside North Vietnam's 12-mile (19.3-km) territorial limit. Suddenly, three North Vietnamese motor torpedo boats were spotted as they approached the destroyer at high speed. The destroyer fired warning shots. When the North Vietnamese craft failed to turn from their apparent attack course, her captain ordered the destroyer's 5-inch (127-mm) main guns to tackle the closing craft, disabling one and hitting another. Even so, the craft fired two torpedoes that passed within 200 yards (118m) of the *Maddox*. The destroyer had radioed the aircraft carrier U.S.S. *Constellation* for support, but the North Vietnamese craft sheered off before the arrival of carrierborne aircraft.

Johnson still refused to be provoked into premature action and said merely that "The United States government expects that North Vietnam will be under no misapprehension as to the grave consequences which would inevitably result from any further unprovoked military action against United States forces."

The Gulf of Tonkin Incident

The following day, the patrol in the Gulf of Tonkin was strengthened by a second destroyer, the U.S.S. *C. Turner Joy*. On August 4, the two destroyers were steaming in international waters when radar reported the approach of five attack craft. The two forces maneuvered against each other, and the two American captains, convinced that their ships were actually under attack, ordered their gunners to open fire and called for air support. It was reported that two of the North Vietnamese craft had been sunk, and another two damaged.

Some American officers later stated their belief that what the *Maddox*'s nexperienced radar operator reported as attackers were in fact radar returns from the turbulent wake of the *C. Turner Joy*. At the time, it seemed certain that the two

Da Nang
For further references
see pages
51, 54, 95, 99

Opposite: American carriers operated on two stations east of the Vietnamese coast, with their tactical aircraft able to strike at targets in any part of the two Vietnams. This is the U.S.S. *Constellation* preparing to take on supplies from the combat stores ship *Niagara Falls*, the third of the seven-strong "Mars" class of underway replenishment ships whose design combined the capabilities of store ships, store issue ships, and aviation store ships, but which had no storage for bulk petroleum products.

warships had come under North Vietnamese attack. Johnson ordered air attacks on the naval bases used by such attackers, and he moved to present his advisers' draft resolution to Congress for approval.

Johnson announced on August 5 that U.S. forces were making measured response to the North Vietnamese aggression, but had no intention of broadening the scope of the existing war. At the same time, tactical aircraft from the carriers U.S.S. *Ticonderoga* and *Constellation* attacked four North Vietnamese naval bases and an oil storage depot, destroying about 25 attack craft and setting fire to 90 percent of the oil stored at Vinh. American losses were two aircraft shot down and two more damaged, all victims of the potent North Vietnamese antiaircraft arm.

American public opinion was strongly behind Johnson's action at this time. On August 7, Congress declared its support for the president's decision to "take all necessary measures to repel any armed attack against the forces of the United States and...to take all necessary steps including the use of armed force to assist any member or protocol state" of the Southeast Asia Treaty Organization.

The Tonkin Resolution

On August 11, Johnson signed the Southeast Asia (Gulf of Tonkin) Resolution. This was considerably short of a declaration of outright war on North Vietnam, but gave the president the right to take whatever action he saw fit. It was a cleverly conceived move. By not declaring war on North Vietnam, Johnson guaranteed that the U.S.S.R. and China were not given to legal grounds to act positively against the United States.

This episode marked the formal entry of the United States into a combat role in the Vietnam War. The event boosted South Vietnamese morale considerably. Ambassador Taylor warned Washington, however, that this would be only temporary and that Khanh's administration was extremely rocky. It was at this stage, though, that on August 16 Khanh declared himself president with wide-

ranging – indeed dictatorial – powers. Taylor was all too correct in his assessment of the South Vietnamese mood; and in late August, a series of riots and demonstrations erupted against the government, which put down an attempted military revolt on September 13 and guaranteed at least its short-term survival by promising an early return to civilian government.

These social and political upheavals in South Vietnam's urban areas were paralleled by events in the central highlands, where the Montagnards made a determined effort to secede from South Vietnam and create their own state, free from the constant discrimination practiced against them by the lowland South Vietnamese. This revolt was brought to an end by an American threat to end Montagnard subsidies.

The continuing military difficulties in South Vietnam combined with the instability of the country's government to bring about a change in the overall American approach to the Vietnam War. The U.S. had previously offered the possibility of joint American and South Vietnamese moves against North Vietnam as a way of keeping the ambitions of South Vietnam's leaders under control. Now, the U.S. shifted steadily to the view that a unilateral American effort against North Vietnam was the only possible way of bolstering South Vietnamese national morale and keeping the country in the war. Within this context, the Joint Chiefs of Staff proposed that U.S. forces engineer an occurrence similar to the Gulf of Tonkin incident to provide a pretext for air attacks on North Vietnam. In this way, the Joint Chiefs of Staff believed, the North Vietnamese would soon realize that it was the scale of their own operations in South Vietnam that determined the level of destruction imposed on them.

President Johnson Reveals his Indecisiveness

Johnson saw considerable merit in the suggestion of the Joint Chiefs of Staff, but refused to consider a concerted bombing campaign against North Vietnamese targets. He did however authorize limited measures designed to put pressure on the North Vietnamese, one-for-one air raids on North Vietnam in response to any North Vietnamese attacks on American units, and a resumption of destroyer patrols off the North Vietnamese coast.

The patrols almost immediately produced another incident in the Gulf of Tonkin: during the night of September 18, the destroyers U.S.S. *Parsons* and U.S.S. *Morton* detected North Vietnamese torpedo boat attacks developing on three separate occasions and responded with 5-inch and 3-inch (76-mm) gunfire. Neither destroyer actually saw the supposed attackers, and Johnson refused to use the incident as the pretext for an air attack on North Vietnam. It was clear that the Gulf of Tonkin was becoming an area of questionable usefulness to the American and South Vietnamese naval effort, and further patrols were canceled. On

October 4 Johnson did authorize another series of covert operations against the North Vietnamese coastal region.

Attack on Bien Hoa Air Base

Throughout October, Johnson resisted pressure for a bombing campaign. He maintained this resistance even after the Viet Cong attacked the U.S. air base at Bien Hoa near Saigon on November 2, killing five Americans and wounding another 76, as well as destroying six Martin B-57 bombers. Two days later, Johnson scored a resounding victory over Senator Barry Goldwater in the 1964 presidential elections, but there was increasing concern in the presidential camp about the number of Americans who were unhappy with Johnson's running of the Vietnam War. It was not clear whether the public wanted an American withdrawal from South Vietnam, or a

For much of the war, the U.S. Air Force was prevented by political considerations from undertaking any type of genuine strategic bombing. For this reason, the Boeing B-52 Stratofortress was available for the tactical role, in which it carried vast weights of ''iron'' bombs for release at high altitude against areas thought to contain Viet Cong and North Vietnamese troops. It was a singularly wasteful application of heavy air power, and the B-52 came to be hated by the communist forces as the silent purveyor of mass destruction.

more vigorous policy designed to win the war. What was becoming abundantly clear, however, was the general dissatisfaction with Johnson's equivocal leadership in the matter. Just before the November 1964 elections, Johnson convened a working group with wide terms of reference and instructed it to assess all the options for United States policy toward Southeast Asia. The working group decided that the best course was a steadily more intense bombing campaign, starting with attacks on the communist infiltration routes of the Ho Chi Minh Trail through Laos and culminating, if necessary, with an increasingly heavy operation against North Vietnam. Johnson himself was not happy to see an escalation of the war, but appreciated the need to bolster the South Vietnamese government and armed forces. Throughout this period, moreover, American intelligence reported that the flow of North Vietnamese men and materiel into South Vietnam was increasing steadily. At the same time, the South Vietnamese government was torn

between rival factions, and the A.R.V.N. was still proving itself completely incapable of stemming the tide of communist tactical successes.

Ambassador Taylor returned to Washington late in November 1964 to urge a more active U.S. participation in an escalated war. Taylor failed to persuade Johnson to accept this course, but he finally convinced the president to accept a compromise: an American bombing campaign against North Vietnam in exchange for an extensive package of reform in South Vietnam. Johnson was still worried about the dangers of escalating the war, however, and authorized only the first steps in this plan, consisting of an intensified air effort against the Ho Chi Minh Trail in Laos and U.S. naval support for clandestine South Vietnamese operations on the North Vietnamese coast. Johnson also instructed Taylor to tell Khanh that joint American and South Vietnamese air attacks on North Vietnam were a possible response to continued communist gains

With bombs from a higher plane visible in the background, a B-52 unloads 1,000- and 750-pound bombs on suspected communist positions 25 miles from Bien Hoa Air Base in December 1966.

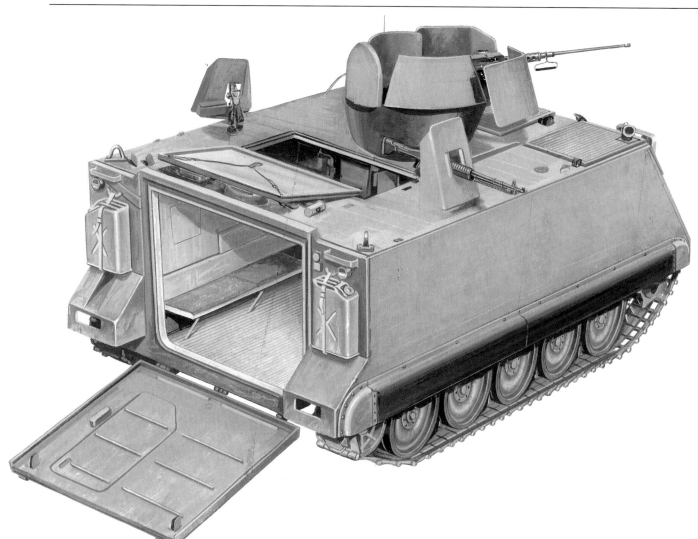

The most important armored personnel carrier fielded by the U.S. forces in South Vietnam was the M113, an all-aluminum craft designed and built by FMC. The type was developed from 1954 as a successor to the unsatisfactory M75 and M59 vehicles. Production began in 1960, and the type was in full service before the beginning of the Vietnam War.

in South Vietnam, but only if the U.S. was confident that the South Vietnamese could handle any upsurge of North Vietnamese activity that this course of action might provoke.

Limited Offensive Operations

The increased air effort over Laos was named Operation "Barrel Roll." It was limited to a weekly maximum of two missions, each by four aircraft, and therefore had absolutely no effect. The same was true of the naval campaign, which had no sooner started than it was halted by the onset of the mon- soon season. The effort to reform the South Vietnamese government was equally abortive. After the riots of August 1964, Khanh had created a High National Council to draft the constitution that

would be adopted by the promised civilian government. This transition was notionally achieved on November 4, 1964, when Khanh supposedly stepped down in favor of a civilian government with Tran Van Huong as its premier. In fact, Khanh remained the power behind the scenes. Huong decided to appoint a cabinet of technicians instead of politicians, and he soon fell foul of the powerful Buddhist and Roman Catholic factions, which wanted a share of power. The adherents of both factions rioted, and though Huong secured military support to suppress the disorder, the days of his administration were num- bered. On December 19, another military revolt took place. The civil government was replaced by an Armed Forces Council, in which Huong was retained as nominal head of government. On January 27, 1965, the Armed Forces Council replaced Huong with Nguyen Khanh, after further Buddhist rioting occurred in response to orders for an increased draft.

Viet Cong Terrorist Outrages

Meanwhile, the Viet Cong had been continuing their terrorist campaign in South Vietnam's larger cities and towns. A notable outrage occurred on December 24, 1964, when the Brink Hotel in Saigon was bombed, resulting the deaths of two Americans and the wounding of 51 Americans and South Vietnamese. Taylor argued that this was the ideal excuse for the beginning of the bombing effort against North Vietnam, but Johnson again refused.

As administration succeeded administration in Saigon, the Viet Cong were steadily consolidating their grasp on the country areas around the South Vietnamese capital. The fighting was increasingly heavy, but in general the Viet Cong prevailed. A typical episode occurred at Binh Gia, an anti-communist village of 6,000 people on the coast north of Saigon. The Viet Cong captured Binh Gia at the end of December 1964 and held the village for four days. Before they pulled out, the Viet Cong had severely handled several South Vietnamese attacks, killing six American advisers as well as 177 South Vietnamese soldiers.

This and similar episodes worried Westmoreland badly, for they seemed to suggest that the Viet Cong were now making the classic small-scale war jump from the hit-and-run actions of guerrilla and small-unit warfare to the larger battles of conventional warfare in which bigger units and eventually formations attack and then hold their gains. Taylor agreed with Westmoreland about the significance of the Battle of Binh Gia and again recommended to Washington that the bombing campaign should be started. Johnson refused once more, but he did authorize the joint American and South Vietnamese planning of such a campaign. The president also responded to a suggestion of Taylor and sent to South Vietnam an observation mission headed by National Security Adviser McGeorge Bundy. This mission concluded that the situation was as poor as Taylor and Westmoreland had been reporting. Indeed, shortly before the mission's departure the Viet Cong attacked the advisory group compound and airstrip at Camp Holloway near Pleiku in the central

Ground personnel at Anderson Air Force Base on Guam load 750-pound bombs onto a B-52 before an attack on a target in North Vietnam. The two underwing pylons were designed for the carriage of Hound Dog stand-off missiles, but the carriage of a weapon beam allowed each of them to support four triplets of 750-pound bombs in addition to the substantial number that could be accommodated in the weapon bay.

highlands. The attack, which came immediately after the "Tet Truce" of February 1 to 6, which marked the Vietnamese New Year, resulted in the deaths of nine Americans and the wounding of more than 100 others.

The raid was probably planned as a deliberate provocation of the United States at a time when Alexei Kosygin, the Soviet premier, was visiting Hanoi. Bundy felt that U.S. retaliation could not be postponed any longer, and he telephoned Johnson to that effect. The president finally agreed and ordered an attack on North Vietnamese targets. The same day, an attack by 49 naval warplanes was launched on a barracks complex at Dong Hoi, just inside the North Vietnamese boundary on the Demilitarized Zone and well away from Hanoi. A companion attack by South Vietnamese aircraft was delayed by the weather, but struck another barracks complex at Vinh the following day in Operation "Flaming Dart I." The president announced the raids to the American people with the words that "we have no choice now but to clear the decks and make absolutely clear our continued determination to back South Vietnam in its fight to maintain its independence."

Renewed Pressure for a Bombing Campaign

Taylor and Bundy urged the president to make this just the first step in a measured campaign of attacks against North Vietnam. On February 10, the Viet Cong bombed a hotel that was being used as a billet for American enlisted men at Qui

Another mainstay of the U.S. air effort in Vietnam was the Republic F-105 Thunderchief. Generally known as the "Thud," this heavyweight single-seater was designed as a strike fighter for European operations, but matured as a capable conventional attack plane over Vietnam. This example is preparing to take on fuel from a Boeing KC-135 Stratotanker.

Nhon. Twenty-three were killed, and a large number who were trapped in the wreckage were injured. Johnson decided that such outrages could not be tolerated any longer and authorized "Flaming Dart II" as a second retaliatory raid. There were two options for the bombing campaign against North Vietnam: the "fast, full squeeze," a rapid campaign of heavy attacks on North Vietnamese targets of military significance, and the "slow squeeze" protracted campaign of escalating attacks designed to show the North Vietnamese that the punishment they were receiving was directly related to the extent of their involvement in South Vietnam.

Johnson chose the latter option, and two days after "Flaming Dart II," he announced the start of Operation "Rolling Thunder" as a series of "measured and limited air actions" against North Vietnamese military targets south of the 19th parallel. The first raid was scheduled for February 20, but was postponed after a South Vietnamese military coup that ousted Khanh in favor of a nominally civilian administration under Phan Huy Quat, another puppet of the South Vietnamese armed forces. Thus, the first "Rolling Thunder" mission was flown on March 2, after the first public admission that U.S. warplanes were operating over North Vietnam was made on February 24.

Operation "Rolling Thunder"

"Rolling Thunder" was planned as an air campaign that could be used to tighten the screws on North Vietnam unless it pulled its men out of South Vietnam and ceased to support the Viet Cong. But the campaign's only real effect was to strengthen the resolve of the North Vietnamese people. At first, Johnson allowed

One of the most fearsome weapons used by American tactical warplanes against suspected communist positions was napalm, a form of jellied gasoline carrying an igniter system.

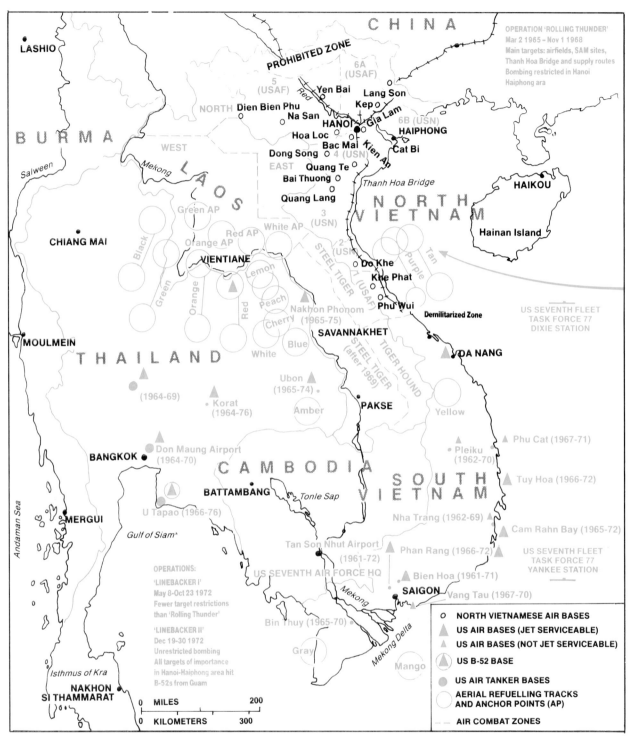

OPERATION 'ROLLING THUNDER'
Mar 2 1965 – Nov 1 1968
Main targets: airfields, SAM sites,
Thanh Hoa Bridge and supply routes
Bombing restricted in Hanoi
Haiphong ara

US SEVENTH FLEET
TASK FORCE 77
DIXIE STATION

US SEVENTH FLEET
TASK FORCE 77
YANKEE STATION

OPERATIONS:
'LINEBACKER I'
May 8–Oct 23 1972
Fewer target restrictions
than 'Rolling Thunder'

'LINEBACKER II'
Dec 19–30 1972
Unrestricted bombing
All targets of importance
in Hanoi-Haiphong area hit
B-52s from Guam

	MILES	200
0		
	KILOMETERS	300
0		

○ NORTH VIETNAMESE AIR BASES
▲ US AIR BASES (JET SERVICEABLE)
▲ US AIR BASES (NOT JET SERVICEABLE)
⊕ US B-52 BASE
● US AIR TANKER BASES
○ AERIAL REFUELLING TRACKS
AND ANCHOR POINTS (AP)
--- AIR COMBAT ZONES

The air war over
Vietnam.

only between two and four raids a week, each undertaken by just a few dozen aircraft. These missions could not deliver enough bomb tonnage to make any impression on the North Vietnamese war effort, but were enough to add a ''considerable and growing risk'' to an already difficult situation.

North Vietnam responded to ''Rolling Thunder'' with the development of a large-scale but centralized air-defense system that eventually embraced manned fighters, surface-to-air missiles, and antiaircraft artillery. Westmoreland rightly believed that this might ''result in mounting casualties as the war goes on –

perhaps more than we will be willing or even able to sustain.''

As Johnson was finally coming to grips with the problem, albeit on a scale far too small to make a major contribution, the situation in South Vietnam was continuing to deteriorate. During the early part of March 1965, the Military Assistance Command, Vietnam, claimed that the current trend, if continued, would result in the South Vietnamese forces being restricted to provincial and district capitals. These places would be so inundated with refugees from Viet Cong-dominated rural areas that they would collapse into anarchy and allow a total Viet Cong victory within 12 months.

Gloomy forecast

This was a realistic but extraordinarily gloomy forecast, and in the first half of 1965, the only hope for salvation lay in U.S. air power. Properly deployed

and controlled, it offered the possibility of hitting North Vietnam hard enough to destroy either its will or its ability to sustain the war, and of cutting the lines of communication by which North Vietnamese reinforcements and supplies reached the Viet Cong. Yet the Qui Nhon and Pleiku episodes seemed to confirm the American apprehension that the A.R.V.N. lacked the capability to protect U.S. air bases in South Vietnam. The Military Assistance Command, Vietnam, calculated that there were 12 Viet Cong battalions, totalling 6,000 men, within striking distance of the vital air base at Da Nang, yet it and its vast stockpiles of essential equipment were protected only by a badly trained A.R.V.N. unit that was most unwilling to undertake even the most elementary patrolling operations.

In February 1965, therefore, it was decided that Da Nang should be protected by U.S. forces. As a first step, a Marine Corps battalion with MIM-23 HAWK (Homing All the Way Killer)

Though it was transferred to South Vietnam, the Raytheon MIM-23 HAWK (Homing All the Way Killer) surface-to-air missile system was not needed, for the North Vietnamese restricted their air force to the defense of North Vietnamese targets against allied air attacks. The first HAWKs were transferred in February 1965 as part of the preparation for the U.S. development of Da Nang into a major base for the expanding U.S. commitment to South Vietnam.

51

Men of the U.S. Marine Corps move up the beach after landing near Da Nang in April 1965. The brigade that arrived in the preceding month marked the beginning of the commitment of American combat forces to the Vietnam War.

surface-to-air missiles was allocated to the base. General John Throckmorton, Westmoreland's deputy, then advised that the base needed a full Marine Expeditionary Brigade of three battalions plus support elements, a request that Westmoreland trimmed to two battalions and forwarded to Washington. This request was endorsed by Taylor and Admiral Ulysses S. Grant Sharp, Commander-in-Chief, Pacific, even though they expressed their concern that the arrival of U.S. ground forces might tempt the A.R.V.N. into leaving as much of the fighting as possible to the Americans, thereby opening the way for an increasing demand for U.S. ground forces in South Vietnam.

American Combat Forces Arrive

Johnson approved the deployment on

Marine, 1st Battalion, 5th Marine Regiment, U.S. Marine Corps, South Vietnam, December 1966.

Operating in the Trung Tin area, this marine sports a mixture of ordinary and jungle kit, including the M1961 webbing rifle belt, the M1955 armor vest, the M1942 first-aid pouch, an electric flashlight with angled head, and the ''duck hunter'' M1 helmet cover of Korean War vintage. The rifle is the standard M14.

LUCAS 91

February 26, and on March 9 Brigadier General Frederick J. Karch's 9th Marine Expeditionary Brigade landed on the beach at Da Nang. It was a decisive moment in the Vietnam War, for the 9th MEB (soon redesignated III Marine Amphibious Force) was the first American combat unit to arrive in South Vietnam.

Westmoreland was worried that within six months the South Vietnamese would hold only "a series of islands of strength clustered around district and provincial capitals" under a government torn between factions wanting to fight on or to reach an accommodation with the communists. Westmoreland's worry was based on the existing military situation in South Vietnam and the knowledge that the first full division of North Vietnamese regulars had infiltrated its way into the central highlands. The arrival of this precursor of a sizable North Vietnamese Army (N.V.A.) contingent in South Vietnam marked the implementa-

tion of a 1964 North Vietnamese plan to reinforce the Viet Cong to a strength that would defeat the A.R.V.N. before large U.S. ground forces had been committed. Westmoreland was therefore right in his assessment that the war was about to enter a new phase in which guerrilla actions by the Viet Cong, with North Vietnamese support, would give way to conventional military confrontations involving North Vietnamese regular forces as well as Viet Cong "main force" units. Westmoreland reckoned that it would take at least a year to train the A.R.V.N. to the level at which it could master the Viet Cong, but thought that he might have only six months left to address a problem complicated considerably by the arrival of North Vietnamese regular forces.

Westmoreland would have liked to create an international force of five divisions to be deployed from the coast of the Sea of China along the Demilitarized Zone and through the Laotian panhandle

A South Vietnamese river group transports an assault group along a small canal, part of the continuous campaign to deny the communists free use of South Vietnam's waterways for movement of men, equipment, and political cadres.

Left: A marine sniper, armed with a Winchester 70 rifle, waits for word from his observer (right) about a possible target.

Below: One of the great but unexpected successes of the Vietnam War was the elderly Douglas A-1 Skyraider attack warplane. The Skyraider received greatest praise for its high warload, endurance, and ability to deliver its weapons at low speed and low altitude with pinpoint accuracy. Seen here during a napalm attack on a suspected Viet Cong position is an A-1E of the U.S. air force 1st Air Commando Squadron.

the section of Laos west and south of Vietnam above and below the Demilitarized Zone where the main part of the Ho Chi Minh trail was located. In Westmoreland's opinion, the creation and deployment of such a force would marshall world opinion against North Vietnamese aggression. Johnson did not approve such a move, and even if he had, it would have taken several months to get the international force into position. Westmoreland did not have several months. The only alternative was to bring in enough U.S. ground forces to hold the line until the revived A.R.V.N. could replace them.

Communist Plans

The presence of a single North Vietnamese division in the central highlands suggested that the communist plan was to cut South Vietnam into two sections, conquer the northern provinces, and then turn on the southern provinces. In the light of this assessment, Westmoreland asked for an American division to hold the central provinces, and for two more battalions of marines to protect the northern provinces' vital air bases for the "Rolling Thunder" campaign. Late in March 1965, Taylor took Westmoreland's

This photograph shows a mortar team of Company "C," 2nd Brigade, 1st Cavalry Division (Airmobile), during a fire mission against Viet Cong positions in February 1966. The mortar proved itself an invaluable weapon in Vietnam, where its high-trajectory, plunging fire was able to drop bombs onto the enemy through the cover of trees.

request to Washington, only to discover that Johnson was still hesitating about an increased U.S. involvement in the Vietnam War and would therefore approve only the two marine battalions.

Taylor then persuaded the president of the advantages inherent in a so-called "enclave policy," which did not meet with Westmoreland's approval. This policy stressed the creation of defensive enclaves around vital air bases and ports, which would have the twin advantages of limiting U.S. involvement while reassuring South Vietnam of the United States' full commitment. Johnson agreed to the creation of such enclaves and allowed their American garrisons to patrol up to a 50-mile (80-km) radius outside the enclave to prevent the concentration of communist attack formations.

Johnson was showing greater signs of indecision, which communicated itself to a high-level meeting held on April 20 in Honolulu between Taylor, Westmoreland, McNamara, and General Earle G. Wheeler, chairman of the Joint Chiefs of Staff. None of those present thought that "Rolling Thunder" would in itself secure decisive results without a significant improvement in the military situation on the ground in South Vietnam. The only way to achieve this end, the conference decided, was to increase the U.S. commitment from four to 13 battalions and to ask for help from

When American forces arrived in large numbers in 1965, the high command gave them a handbook. It told them what to expect from the enemy, and how to behave around Vietnamese civilians.

The VC is an elusive and determined foe. He is well organized politically and militarily, and employs both conventional and guerrilla tactics. He is an expert in the arts of camouflage, deception and ambush. He is a hardy and ruthless fighter, but not an invincible one. He can and will be defeated.

WINNING AND MAINTAINING CIVILIAN SUPPORT
1. General
Winning and maintaining the friendship and cooperation of the Vietnamese civilians living within the operational area is an essential step in reducing the effectiveness of the local Viet Cong guerillas – they cannot operate effectively without civilian support. The two main aspects of our military presence which contribute towards good civil-military relations are the individual soldier's positive attitude in his dealings with local civilians, and the planned civil actions of military units.

2. Individual Behaviour
The Viet Cong attempt to separate our soldiers from the local civilians by showing that we are cruel, unthinking, and not concerned with the welfare of the local peoples. The VC can be defeated in these efforts by the strength and generosity we show in our daily lives. The "Nine Rules" for the military man in Vietnam provide the guide for doing this. They are:

a. Remember we are guests here: We make no demands and seek no special treatment.

b. Join the people: Understand their life, use phrases from their language and honor their customs and laws.

c. Treat women with politeness and respect.

d. Make friends among the soldiers and common people.

e. Always give the Vietnamese the right of way.

f. Be alert to security and ready to react with your military skill.

g. Do not attract attention by loud, rude or unusual behaviour.

h. Avoid separating ourselves from the people by a display of wealth or privilige.

i. Above all else, we are members of the US military forces on a difficult mission, responsible for all our official and personal actions. Reflect honor upon ourselves and the United States of America.

These are typical lowland conditions for Vietnam, with rice paddies set among heavy semi-tropical vegetation, as men of the 2nd Battalion, 7th Regiment, 1st Cavalry Division (Airmobile) patrol during January 1966.

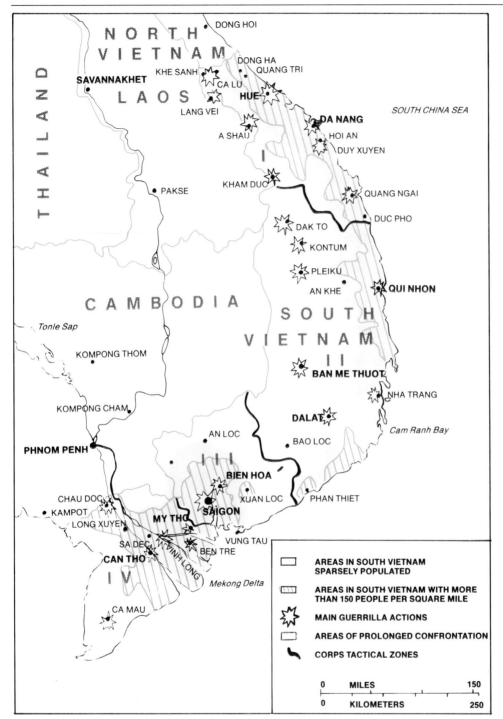

The overall situation in Vietnam during the U.S. commitment to this long-lasting war.

	AREAS IN SOUTH VIETNAM SPARSELY POPULATED
	AREAS IN SOUTH VIETNAM WITH MORE THAN 150 PEOPLE PER SQUARE MILE
	MAIN GUERRILLA ACTIONS
	AREAS OF PROLONGED CONFRONTATION
	CORPS TACTICAL ZONES

| 0 | MILES | 150 |
| 0 | KILOMETERS | 250 |

other interested parties, most notably Australia, New Zealand, and South Korea.

International Support for South Vietnam

As far back as the 1961 "More Flags" program, it had been suggested that the members of the Southeast Asia Treaty Organization should be asked to help. Only Australia and New Zealand responded positively at the time, and they sent advisers as the first elements of forces that totaled 7,000 and 550 respectively by 1969. Three other nations that later contributed combat forces were the Philippines, South Korea, and Thailand, and the peak strength of such "interested party" contin-

gents in 1969 was 68,900, including small detachments supplied by Spain and Taiwan. Non-combat support elements were provided by 34 countries.

The two largest contingents were, of course, those of the United States and South Vietnam. For a host of political and cultural reasons, the South Vietnamese could not serve under American command, and the American public would never have stood for the deployment of U.S. forces under South Vietnamese command. Therefore, two separate but parallel command structures evolved for the South Vietnamese and American forces.

As the head of the Military Assistance Command, Vietnam, Westmoreland controlled all operations in South Vietnam, as well as tactical air operations in Laos and the portion of North Vietnam just above the Demilitarized Zone. In his capacity as Commander-in-Chief, Pacific, Admiral Sharp controlled all other air operations over North Vietnam. Sharp also supervised the activities of the 7th Fleet, though Westmoreland had tactical command of carrierborne aircraft in South Vietnam. When Boeing B-52 Stratofortress heavy bombers were added to the inventory of weapons deployed in the theater, they were controlled by the U.S. Air Force's Strategic Air Command, although the designation of targets was the responsibility of Westmoreland but subject to approval by Washington.

Parallel American and South Vietnamese Commands

As the American commitment in South Vietnam grew, Westmoreland developed

Fixed installations such as airfields and fuel dumps were natural targets for the Viet Cong. Here, a fireman sprays firefighting chemicals on burning fuel at a South Vietnamese depot after a Viet Cong mortar attack.

General William C. Westmoreland had the ultimately thankless task of heading the U.S. Military Assistance Command, Vietnam, in the period between 1964 and 1968, when he returned to the United States as Army Chief of Staff until his retirement in 1972.

the structure to include commands such as the U.S. Army, Vietnam (primarily an administrative and logistical echelon), the 7th Air Force, and the Naval Force, Vietnam. The A.R.V.N. had already divided South Vietnam into four "corps tactical zones," and Westmoreland established three parallel commands. In the I Corps Tactical Zone, covering the northern provinces, the U.S. counterpart was the III Marine Amphibious Force; in the II Corps Tactical Zone, covering the central provinces, it was the I Field Force. In the III Corps Tactical Zone, covering the provinces around Saigon, it was the II Field Force. The very few U.S. troops in the IV Corps Tactical Zone, covering the southern provinces, came under the control of the senior American adviser to the commander of the South Vietnamese IV Corps.

The nine extra battalions approved by Johnson arrived in South Vietnam during May and June 1965. The "enclave strategy" came to an end as Westmoreland's forces were permitted to undertake "counter-insurgency combat operations." This change was not revealed to the American public for fear of an adverse reaction, even though it was

Above: An alert crewman mans the door-mounted M60 machine gun aboard a Sikorsky UH- 34E Seahorse helicopter of the U.S. Marine Corps over Vietnam.

Right: This is one of the classic photographs to emerge from the Vietnam War. A Douglas A-1E Skyraider of the U.S. Air Force climbs sharply after dropping a white phosphorus incendiary bomb on a Viet Cong target.

Right: Operational conditions in South Vietnam often made normal procedures impossible and emphasized the need for the troops to use their own initiative in matters such as keeping clean.

Below: Though the "Huey" was the most numerous helicopter in Vietnam by far, larger machines such as this twin-rotor Boeing Vertol CH-47A Chinook offered far greater lift capability. The Chinook's greatest importance, however, was not as a troop transport, but as a logistical transport, bringing in ammunition and other supplies to artillery fire bases, and acting as a rescue helicopter for the crew of downed aircraft.

Left: Men of the 1st Cavalry Division (Airmobile) fire on a Viet Cong bunker during Operation "Masher" in January 1966.

Below: Air attacks could have a devastating effect on the communists, but they also destroyed much of South Vietnam's tree population. Tangled trunks and foliage, such as this near Bong Son in Operation "Masher," made it difficult for the men of the 1st Cavalry Division to sweep through the area after the attack to make sure that there were no surviving pockets of resistance.

Right: A vehicle that proved its worth in the Vietnam War was the hovercraft, which was used by the U.S. Navy as the PACV (Patrol Air-Cushion Vehicle) to sweep through South Vietnam's extremely shallow coastal waters in pursuit of communist infiltrators.

Below: A force of South Vietnamese riverine craft patrols a typical waterway of the country's waterlogged southern region.

patently obvious to U.S. media personnel in South Vietnam that U.S. combat forces most certainly were not limited to the defensive enclaves as publicly claimed by the administration. The administration's manifest lie created an inevitable, most unfortunate "credibility gap" between the administration and the media, and by extension the American people. It was to bedevil the conduct of the war in its later stages.

Growing Communist Strength

It would be some time before the newly arrived American units could make their presence felt, and in the meantime the Viet Cong continued to gather strength. Attacks in regimental strength were now common, and the communists overran several provincial capitals, destroyed a complete A.R.V.N. battalion in a cleverly constructed and well-executed ambush,

and besieged an outpost in the central highlands. They were clear tokens that the war had moved out of its guerrilla phase, yet the attention of the American force was caught more by the oddly slow performance of the North Vietnamese division in the central highlands than by the emergence of the Viet Cong as a conventional fighting force.

South Vietnam itself continued to lurch from one political crisis to another. In May 1965 there was an attempted coup, and in response Quat tried to reshuffle his cabinet. This failed and Quat resigned, turning the government over to the military who were already the real rulers of South Vietnam. The military established a ten-man Committee for the Direction of the State with Air Vice Marshal Ky as premier and General Nguyen Van Thieu as head of state. Although there was little evidence for it at the time, this new administration at last began to bring a measure of stability into

A UH-34E helicopter lands men of the U.S. Marine Corps during Operation "Colorado" in August 1966.

An infantry platoon on a search and destroy mission three kilometers west of Duc Pho. An armored UH-1B helicopter prepares to land troops into an area where a suspected Viet Cong outpost was located.

Below: Worried by the possibility of communist mines and traps, men of a marine patrol move with extreme caution.

The U.S. Air Force's main rescue helicopter in the Vietnam War was the Sikorsky HH-3E, a development of the Sea King naval helicopter that received the approving nickname "Jolly Green Giant." In addition to specialized electronics, the HH-3A had armor protection, armament, self-sealing fuel tanks, inflight refueling capability, and provision for drop tanks. The result was a machine that could enter areas defended by communist antiaircraft weapons to rescue downed American airmen.

South Vietnam's turbulent political life.

Westmoreland thought that the new government would last no longer than its predecessors, and he was faced with the continuing deterioration of the A.R.V.N., which was losing battalions more quickly than replacement units could be created. Westmoreland noted that a favorite Viet Cong and North Vietnamese tactic was to draw A.R.V.N. units away from centers of population. These areas were then easier prey for the communist terror and propaganda campaign that was continuing unabated. Westmoreland decided to use American units to contain the communist field forces, leaving the A.R.V.N. free to protect South Vietnam's urban areas. The U.S. commander, still thinking in terms of shoring up South Vietnam until it was strong enough to undertake its own protection, asked for a total strength of 34 U.S. and ten allied battalions. This total, Westmoreland reasoned, would not be enough to win the war but would buy South Vietnam the time it needed, with U.S. support, to revive the A.R.V.N. as an effective fighting force.

Ambiguous Authorization

Westmoreland's proposal called for a considerable expansion of the American commitment and was the subject of much debate in Washington. Given the delay imposed by this debate, Johnson authorized Westmoreland to use American troops in situations that might "strengthen the relative position" of the South Vietnamese. Johnson's authorization did not differentiate between offensive or defensive strengthening, and Westmoreland saw in it his chance to undertake the first large U.S. operation of the war. This was a raid into a communist sanctuary area west of Saigon, in a sector known as War Zone D, close to the American air base at Bien Hoa.

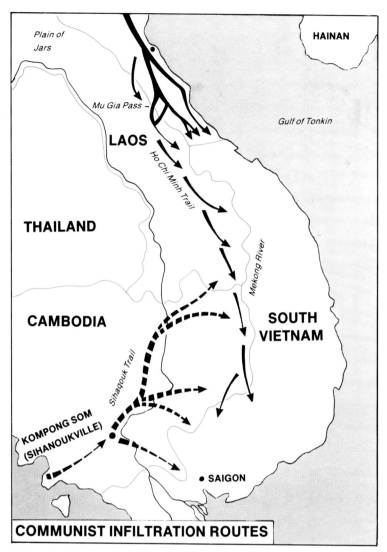

COMMUNIST INFILTRATION ROUTES

Above: Communist infiltration routes into South Vietnam.

Right: Though it entered service as the U.S. Air Force's first supersonic interceptor, the North American F-100 Super Sabre saw most of its service in Vietnam as a fighter bomber and proved itself able to deliver its weapons with considerable accuracy while surviving considerable battle damage.

An eight-battalion U.S., Australian, New Zealand, and South Vietnamese force was created on the basis of the U.S. 173rd Airborne Brigade. As this force moved through War Zone D after the operation began on June 27, 1965, there were several sharp actions with communist forces, but none was any more conclusive than the operation as a whole. While still considering Westmoreland's request for more troops, Johnson sent to South Vietnam a "fact-finding team" of the type that soon became commonplace in this Washington-run war. The team consisted of McNamara and Henry Cabot Lodge, the latter soon to succeed Taylor in a second tour as American ambassador to Saigon. Westmoreland informed McNamara and Lodge that his intention was still to stabilize the situation in South Vietnam. For this, he needed 175,000 American troops in the short term, with another 100,000 to follow so that the situation in South Vietnam could be retrieved before the end of 1965. He would then undertake a major offensive in 1966 and eliminate communist forces in South Vietnam within 18 months.

Large-scale Commitment

McNamara and the Joint Chiefs of Staff supported Westmoreland's plan, and despite growing opposition in

Washington to this apparently open-ended commitment, Johnson announced on July 28 that "I have today ordered to Vietnam the Airmobile Division [the recently formed 1st Cavalry Division (Airmobile)] and certain other forces which will raise our fighting strength from 75,000 to 125,000 men almost immediately. Additional forces will be needed later, and they will be sent as requested." The announcement marked a key decision in the American commitment to the Vietnam War, for it revealed a formal involvement without limits in terms of numbers of men and months.

Not unnaturally, Westmoreland's operational thinking was colored by his assessment of the situation in South Vietnam. He saw it as crumbling structure currently under attack by the Viet Cong, with the North Vietnamese Army waiting in the wings to deliver the decisive blow as soon as the Viet Cong had destabilized South Vietnam's underlying political, social, and military foundations sufficiently. In this situation, Westmoreland reasoned, the first task was to drive away the North Vietnamese so that the Americans and South Vietnamese would not have to keep a constant watch over their shoulders as they then eliminated the Viet Cong. Thus it would be the task of the Americans to fight the N.V.A. The A.R.V.N. would tackle the Viet Cong, and the South Vietnamese government would improve the country's political, economic, and social backgrounds with the support of various American agencies.

An automatic rifleman with the 3rd Squadron, 1st Platoon, Company "C," 1st Battalion, 18th Infantry Regiment of the 1st Infantry Division, PFC. Frederick G. Culp wades across a river east of Saigon during a search- and-destroy mission in April 1966.

This Cessna A-37B Dragonfly, a dedicated light attack derivative of the U.S. Air Force's T-37 "Tweet" trainer sports the markings of a unit in the South Vietnamese Air Force. The "Tweet" concept was proved with a single YAT-38D prototype converted from a T-37B, and then service trials were undertaken in Vietnam with 39 examples of the A-37A "production" conversion of the T-37B. These tests confirmed that the Dragonfly had very useful capabilities, and 577 aircraft were built to the improved A-37B standard with a reengineered airframe able to accept more powerful engines and larger underwing loads. The two-seat A-37B was powered by two 2,850-pound thrust General Electric J85-GE-17A non-afterburning turbojets. At a maximum weight of 14,000 pounds, it could carry an armament of one 0·3-in (7·62-mm) six-barrel Minigun with 1,500 rounds of ammunition and, on eight underwing hardpoints, 5,000 pounds or more of disposable stores such as "iron" bombs, retarded bombs, cluster bombs, napalm bombs, bomblet dispensers, gun pods, and rocket launchers. The model had a maximum speed of 507 miles per hour at an altitude of 16,000 feet, and its span was 35 feet 10½ inches. Other features were an inflight refueling probe and flak curtains inside the cockpit area to protect the crew from shell fragments and small-arms fire.

Westmoreland's Three-phase Strategy

Within this basic scheme, Westmoreland planned a three-phase strategy. In the first phase, U.S. forces would protect the large number of logistical bases that would have to be developed all over South Vietnam to support later operations. If these bases were threatened by the North Vietnamese, American units would be committed to offensive operations designed to clear the area. In the second phase, the Americans would drive into the hinterland of South Vietnam with the objective of destroying communist bases and sanctuaries, bringing the enemy forces into battle, and inflicting heavy losses on them. And in the third phase, the Americans would launch sustained operations against the N.V.A. forces in South Vietnam, either destroying them or so weakening them that the A.R.V.N. would be able to contain and then eliminate them with decreasing U.S. assistance.

Westmoreland relied on U.S. troops to fight the N.V.A. because the firepower and mobility of the American units were greater than those of comparable A.R.V.N. units, because that firepower could be moved more readily to the remoter areas where the N.V.A. lurked, and because it was thought better for the A.R.V.N. to play the more dominant role in the populated areas where the Viet Cong generally operated. Even so, Westmoreland planned for U.S. troops to operate in heavily populated regions where there were strong concentrations of communist forces.

Westmoreland knew that obvious step of sealing South Vietnam's 900-mile land border with Cambodia, Laos, and North Vietnam was impossible. He lacked the manpower for the task, which would in any case have been all but impossible because of the nature of the terrain and

Men of the 2nd Battalion, 503rd Airborne Infantry Regiment, 173rd Airborne Brigade, wait to board their helicopter as a UH-1D lifts off for a search-and-destroy operation northwest of Bien Hoa in November 1966.

Right: As the South Vietnamese Air Force lacked significant airlift capability, the movement of men such as these South Vietnamese had to be undertaken by the U.S. Air Force, in this instance with a Fairchild C-123 Provider. This light transport was powered by twin piston engines, and its short take-off and landing capability made it especially valuable for shuttling men and supplies into and out of small forward airfields.

Below: South Vietnam's lack of significant airlift capacity also meant that the U.S. Air Force was entrusted with larger-scale movements, such as that of these South Vietnamese infantrymen, in the Lockheed C-1309 Hercules. Although this plane was powered by four turboprop engines, it was still able to operate into and out of small airstrips.

Opposite Top: A marine dog handler moves into a suspect village during Operation "Orange" in March 1966. Dogs proved very useful "weapons" in the allied effort to discover Viet Cong guerrillas lurking in concealed positions.

Opposite Bottom: Men of the 3rd Marines establish the multichannel radio link that allowed dispersed units such as this one to stay in contact with other units in the area as well as higher headquarters.

Before the American intervention, Communist forces had been about to conquer South Vietnam. The tremendous American mobility and firepower stunned the Communists. A captured diary describes what it was like:

23 October 1965

While I am writing this diary, the enemy aircraft are hovering low over. There are times they stoop down to tree-tops level but they do not see anything. By now the whole platoon is waiting for the order to begin the assault. All necessary equipment is at hand and once the order is given, let's go. Will there be a fight or will we be again waiting and waiting as the other day? I again hope that this afternoon I will have the opportunity to register some success in the diary. At noon today, the enemy aircraft conducted a heavy airstrike in the village in the rear of the battlefield. We could hear very distinctly the noise made by their bombs and rockets.

We spent all day long yesterday to keep waiting as we are doing now. Suddenly at half past two the order for departure was given. I thought that "this is it" but it was only an alert: the battalion ordered us to dig alternative positions. We finished the work at 7 o'clock. On their way back to our primary positions, it was very dark and we strayed for a long time.

24 October 1965

At last we met them! On 23 October, at half past four the enemy fell into our battlefield. My unit received the order to assault. When we approached the route, friendly units had already opened fire. When we arrived upto the top of the Doc Lap Hill, we discovered an enemy observation post; the enemy soldiers were digging their positions. The enemy fired intensely. They made use of all their weapons. We kept quiet. When the shooting was over my platoon was ordered to move forward along the left side of the route, we stopped and waited for the order to open fire. No order was given. Two of our men were sent to establish contact. Unfortunately they strayed and we lay there until dawn. We were planning to withdraw when suddenly we received a volley of machine gun fire and a mortar shell from the enemy. We suffered 5 casualties, among them the platoon leader, and a recruit who had his left arm torn off. We immediately gave them first aid and withdrew. We reached our unit at 7 p.m. We had strayed for one day and one night and had

eaten during this time only drycooked rice. Three of our comrades are still missing.

26 October 1965

My unit moves to another place. With those who remain, we form a squad, integrated into a friendly platoon to prepare for combat. With those who come back from the evacuation of wounded we also form another squad and keep ready for the mission. But all day long we find nothing. In the sky the aircraft keep flying, numberless and incessantly. Our former positions are hit by airstrikes, there are no casualties but some of our equipment which we still leave the is damaged. At 6 o'clock I cross the route with the sixth squad to pick up the friendly platoon on the other side. It is not until 2 o'clock in the morning that we finally come back. We do not eat anything and just sleep. At dawn we hurriedly prepare to coordinate with the C company. The enemy aircraft keep flying; the helicopters lower themselves to the tree-tops in flocks; the jets too and the Dakotas as well.

29 October 1965

And so the month of October is nearly over. Time has run too fast and we just have only a fighting. We have been waiting for the enemy but until 11 o'clock this morning, we still have zero as results. At half past four yesterday afternoon, we were ordered to depart. At the same time it began to rain. It would be a good opportunity for us to conduct the attack. We were only at midway when we were ordered to stop. Then suddenly we were ordered to move back! What a sad thing! One after the other our columns returned to our point of departure. We had just begun to sleep when warning orders for an attack were given. But finally nothing happened. At 5 o'clock we were again on the move. At midway we withdrew then advanced anew. When we were near the battlefield, the enemy was already there. It was the first time that I saw the M113 APC's but not very distinctly. These vehicles were in columns along the route while the enemy troops were moving around. This time there would be a big fight; we did noting but wait. Then suddenly and finally, we were ordered to withdraw to leave the job to the recoilless rifles and mortar elements. When we reached our positions, still nothing happened. A moment later the recoilless rifles and mortar elements also went back. The results still remained a zero. What a discouraging situation! Two times already! What are the higher echelons planning to do! We are kept in readiness for an eventual attack.

Left: As the rest of the platoon spread out in preparation for an attack, the M60 machine gun team of the 2nd Platoon, Company "E," 2nd Battalion, 4th Marine Regiment keeps the enemy pinned down near Chu Lai in January 1966.

Below: South Vietnamese paratroopers descend from a C-123 light transport after being dropped near Cau Mong in March 1966.

its thick vegetation. The U.S. commander instead decided to rely mainly on air reconnaissance, long-range patrols, and a network of strategically placed outposts manned by men of the ethnic minority groups living in these border regions. A combination of these three factors, Westmoreland thought, would inevitably detect communist infiltrators, especially those of N.V.A. formations, who could then be tackled by long-range surface bombardment, tactical air power, and U.S. combat forces moved into the area by fixed- and/or rotary-winged aircraft.

An International Force?

Westmoreland still hoped that an international force could be created to hold the Demilitarized Zone. He anticipated that he could then use his own forces to strike into southeastern Laos and sever the Ho Chi Minh Trail. In the short term, however, Westmoreland thought that he lacked the strength for this undertaking and therefore did not press Washington for permission for a Laotian move. By 1968, when the general finally thought that his forces were strong enough, President Johnson

These Viet Cong suspects were seized in September 1966, only 18 miles northwest of Saigon, with the aid of a ''counter-terrorist'' unit of ex-members of the Viet Cong working with the 2nd Battalion, 27th Infantry Regiment, 25th Infantry Division.

Left: White phosphorus mortar bombs burst in the type of forest much favored by the Viet Cong as a base area.

Below: Men of the 2nd Battalion, 5th Marine Regiment, board their helicopter for movement into a search-and-destroy area. Operating in the northern part of South Vietnam, the marines had to face the possibility of a North Vietnamese invasion across the Demilitarized Zone, as well as the normal hazards of Viet Cong missions in their operational region.

was committed to a policy of containing the war in Vietnam and refused to authorize any attack into Laos.

The nature of the country and the lack of sizable U.S. combat forces therefore forced Westmoreland to adopt what was in effect a strategy of attrition. U.S. troops waited for the communists to come to them, only then responding in a way designed to destroy very large parts of these forces and break down their cohesion as effective fighting units. Westmoreland knew that the process would be a long one, but he also knew that the A.R.V.N. needed this time to revive itself, regain control of South Vietnam's vital agricultural and urban areas, and starve the Viet Cong of the recruits it

Top: Men of the 101st Airborne Division beat off a Viet Cong attack on their position near Tumorang during Operation ''Hawthorne'' in June 1966.

Below: An American up-country fire base comes under communist attack. Such assaults were commonplace, and the bases were designed and constructed with accommodation, ammunition dumps, and other essentials under protection that could withstand the effect of the comparatively light weapons used by the Viet Cong.

Top: U.S. forces in Vietnam had a huge technical superiority over the Viet Cong, but it became increasingly clear that the firepower and range of weapons such as these 105-mm (4.13-inch) howitzers were of relatively little use against a concealed enemy whose position often could not be fixed with any real accuracy.

Below: A Vietnamese village burns brightly as the men of the 1st Battalion, 5th Marine Regiment, pull out of this region of Tam Ky province on the closing stages of Operation "Colorado." This was the scene of the heaviest fighting in the operation, and on August 10 the marines claimed 114 Viet Cong killed.

needed for continued survival. If the Viet Cong could be brought under control by the A.R.V.N., the only enemy would be the N.V.A. This army, organized and trained on more conventional military lines, could therefore be tackled in standard ways.

Within this overall scheme, Westmoreland planned to locate American divisions and brigades in semi-permanent base camps that would be the core of each formation's area of tactical responsibility. Operations would often compel each of these formations to leave its camps, which would then be held by a small security detachment. In the field, each formation would create a temporary camp, and in the gap between itself and approaching communist forces,

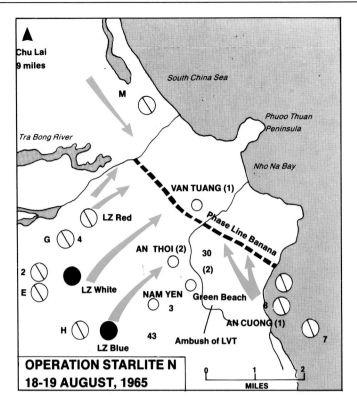

**OPERATION STARLITE N
18-19 AUGUST, 1965**

Map labels:
Chu Lai 9 miles
South China Sea
Tra Bong River
Phuoo Thuan Peninsula
Nho Na Bay
M
VAN TUANG (1)
LZ Red
Phase Line Banana
G 4
AN THOI (2)
30
(2)
2
E
LZ White
NAM YEN
3
Green Beach
8
H
AN CUONG (1)
43
Ambush of LVT
7
LZ Blue
0 1 2
MILES

Opposite Top: One of the most important riverine craft operated by the U.S. Navy in South Vietnam was the PCF (Patrol Craft, Fast). The armament varied, but this boat has a fairly typical fit of two 0·5-inch (12·7-mm) heavy machine guns in a twin mounting above the conning position, and on the after decking a combined mounting for one 0·5-inch heavy machine gun and one 81-mm (3·2-inch) mortar. This latter mounting is covered by a tarpaulin on the boat illustrated.

Opposite Bottom: Another type of craft that proved useful in the delta of the Mekong River was the airboat. Here men of the 5th Special Forces Group train South Vietnamese in the use of the airboat, of which the first 30 were delivered in November 1966.

Left: Undertaken between August 18 and 24, 1965, Operation "Starlite" was the first regimental-size battle fought by U.S. forces since the Korean War.

Below: It was difficult for troops to maintain good health and peak physical condition when they were forced to operate in swamp areas such as this, in the Long Thanh area east of Saigon, where a search-and-destroy operation was mounted in February 1967.

Top: An American minesweeping boat patrols the River Long Tau. Minesweeping was a task that needed to be undertaken on a daily basis to keep this waterway open for supplies moving down to the port of Saigon.

Below: Men of the 1st Battalion, 26th Marine Regiment, are partially silhouetted by the flames of a burning village, the result of never-ending missions to search out and destroy the Viet Cong. This was an episode from Operation ''Deckhouse II'' southeast of Saigon in August 1966.

fire-support bases equipped for all-round defense would be set up. These fire-support bases were intended to accommodate heavy artillery that could furnish long-range support for patrols which would sweep the area around the base. When necessary, companies, battalions, and even regiments would respond to intelligence warnings with "search and destroy" sweeps designed to bring the communists to battle.

One of the reasons for the use of U.S. combat forces in the remote, less heavily populated regions of South Vietnam was to avoid collateral damage to South Vietnamese villages. Even so, it was understood that damage might on occasion be caused if, for example, the communists prepared a defensive position in a village. In these circumstances, the Americans planned to destroy the villages and relocate the villagers. The vacated area could then become a "free-fire zone" into which heavy artillery fire could be called without fears of killing civilians, who might later be permitted to return after the communists had been eliminated. This was admitted to be a harsh policy, but the alternatives, fighting among the civilian population or leaving the communists in control, were both impossible.

The First Major American Action

The first time that U.S. forces became involved in large-scale action was in August 1965 and involved men of Major General Lewis W. Walt's III Marine Amphibious Force. While protecting the airfield at Chu Lai on the north-central coast, the marines discovered a Viet Cong regiment on the Van Tuonf peninsula, only 15 miles from Chu Lai. Operation "Starlite" involved some 4,000 marines in an air- and sea-launched sweep that resulted in the deaths of 700 Viet Cong for the loss of 50 marines killed and 150 wounded. The survivors of the Viet Cong regiment escaped inland to the mountains.

It was an auspicious start, but as was to be the case so often in the Vietnam War, it proved to be a wasted effort except in attritional terms. The marines lacked the strength to garrison the peninsula

Above: A soldier of the 7th Cavalry Regiment, 1st Cavalry Division (Airmobile), searches the debris of a village hit by a major air attack in Operation "Masher" during January 1966. The Viet Cong were absolute masters in the art of building strong bunkers out of locally available materials that helped the structure blend unobtrusively into its surroundings.

Below: Though the Vietnam War was enormously costly to the American taxpayer, considerable sums were saved by the rescue and repair of damaged equipment. Here a Boeing Vertol CH-46A Sea Knight twin-rotor helicopter lifts to safety the fuselage of a Sikorsky UH-34 single-rotor helicopter knocked down in the opening stages of Operation "Colorado" in August 1966.

and therefore pulled out after "Starlite." The communists eventually returned, and in the years to come, the operation had to be repeated on several occasions.

Revised Communist Strategy

As this and other early operations got underway, the threat of the N.V.A. division in the central highlands was developing steadily. It soon became clear that Westmoreland had probably been right in his assessment of a communist effort to split South Vietnam into northern and southern halves. In October 1965, 6,000 N.V.A. soldiers began to gather around the A.R.V.N. outpost at Plei Me, close to the border. The N.V.A. plan was clearly to take Plei Me, then two nearby outposts, to take the provincial capital of Pleiku, and then drive east along Highway 19 to the coast.

The 1st Cavalry Division was deployed to the Highway 19 area and built its base camp at An Khe. Westmoreland's plan

was to use at least part of the division against the communist concentration. With strong support from U.S. tactical aircraft, the A.R.V.N. defeated the N.V.A. attack against Plei Me, and Westmoreland then decided to strike at the N.V.A. concentration in the nearby valley of the Ia Drang River.

The Battle of the Ia Drang Valley

One brigade of the 1st Cavalry Division was committed with exceptionally strong helicopter strength, and this brigade both found and fixed the enemy. This brigade was then lifted out and replaced by another, and the N.V.A. decided to fight it out. Between November 14 and 19, the N.V.A. launched several determined attacks and was driven back on each occasion without making the slightest impression on the American brigade's position. At the same time, U.S. tactical air power, including Boeing B-52 Stratofortress heavy bombers used for the first time, struck at the N.V.A.'s supposed concentration area. It was the first time that American and North Vietnamese forces had met in a major engagement, and at the tactical level, the Ia Drang operation was a major American success. The Americans lost 240 dead, but the N.V.A. lost an estimated 1,800 killed.

What soon became clear, however, was that the N.V.A. division had not been destroyed but had retreated over the frontier into Cambodia. The U.S. forces were forbidden to pursue, and the N.V.A. force was soon restored to full strength and maximum combat capability. This ploy was used frequently by the communist forces, for they soon knew that U.S. ground forces were specifically forbidden to operate in Laos and Cambodia. The most that they were allowed was the despatch of patrols into the area just inside Laos to find concentrations against which tactical air power could be used.

Operation "Market Time"

The infiltration of men and equipment into South Vietnam from North Vietnam was concentrated on the Ho Chi Minh Trail, but a considerable communist effort was made along the coast. From the spring of 1965, Operation "Market Time" was undertaken to check this flow. By the end of 1966, more than 30 U.S. Coast Guard cutters and several hundred South Vietnamese junks were on constant patrol to search any junk or barge that aroused suspicion. Farther from the coast, U.S. naval destroyers and minesweepers formed an outer cordon. An associated program took place on South Vietnam's mass of inland waterways, where more than 100 river patrol craft checked 2,000 or more junks and sampans every day. These twin efforts did not deny waterborne communications to the communists, but they certainly hindered them and made it more difficult to transport men or equipment, and to use small waterborne forces to control the civilian population. One unfortunate effect of this partial success was the diversion of the North Vietnamese effort to the Ho Chi Minh Trail and, as a later addition, the so-called Sihanouk Trail leading from the Cambodian port of Sihanoukville through southeastern Cambodia into the southwestern part of South Vietnam.

By the end of 1965, the strength of the U.S. force in South Vietnam had climbed to 181,000, including three combat divisions (one infantry, one airmobile, and one marine), three army brigades, one marine regiment, and three tactical fighter wings of the air force. There was also a contingent of 20,000 South Koreans (one division and one marine brigade), an Australian battalion, and smaller detachments from New Zealand, the Philippines, Taiwan, and Thailand. This last allied contingent eventually totaled 11,600 men in six battalions by 1970.

A Huge Logistical Effort

The increased U.S. combat commitment was paralleled by a vast and impressive logistical effort. Within 30 months, deliveries from the United States supported a force of 1,300,000, including nearly 500,000 U.S. troops. The average monthly delivery totaled 760,000 tons – 10 million field rations, 71,000 tons of munitions, and 80 million gallons of petroleum fuel. There were greatly expanded or even completely new port facilities in six places. The engineers were also very active within South Vietnam, creating 4 million square yards of aircraft operating area, 2.22 million square yards of storage area (covered and uncovered),

500,000 cubic feet of refrigerated storage, 1,700 miles of road, 5,000 yards of bridge, and 15 fortified base camps.

Among the many oddities of the Vietnam War were its large number of ceasefires, some of them traditional and others official. Of the traditional ceasefires, the most important were those marking Christmas, New Year, the Buddha's birthday, and the lunar new year, known as the Tet, which lasted from February 1 to 6. These ceasefires were never complete, but the communists were astute enough to appreciate that if they conducted any large-scale operations in this period, they would give an important propaganda weapon to the South Vietnamese. Of the official ceasefires, the most important were pauses in the American bombing of North Vietnam, supposedly to provide the North Vietnamese authorities with a respite in which to consider the advantages of negotiation. In reality, neither the administration nor the military believed that the pauses would achieve anything, but the administration ordered them to appease pacifist elements at home and abroad.

The Bombing Pauses

In all, there were eight such pauses in the bombing between 1965 and 1968, but it has become clear that at no stage did the North Vietnamese ever seriously consider

The strain and fatigue of combat operations in South Vietnam are fully evident on the face of this soldier.

Above: This M60 machine gun crew is in action on Hill 170, another of the many small South Vietnamese rises known just by its height in meters, during Operation "Essex" in 1967.

Left: A soldier of the 2nd Battalion, 27th Infantry Regiment, 2nd Brigade, 25th Infantry Regiment, blasts a possible Viet Cong lair with his 12-gauge shotgun during Operation "Junction City" in February 1967.

Long-range artillery support was effective against area targets, and this 175-mm (6·89-in) gun of Battery ''C,'' 2nd Battalion, 32nd Artillery Regiment, is being loaded for such a task in Operation ''Junction City.''

Above: Men of the 5th Marine Regiment crawl forward through thick elephant grass under heavy communist fire about 6 miles south of Da Nang in January 1967 during a joint American and South Korean operation.

Below: A marine lines up a target in the sight of his 106-mm (4·17-inch) recoilless rifle, which is also topped by a 0·5-inch (12·7-mm) spotting rifle. Though this weapon was designed for antitank use, it also proved to be an effective bunker-buster.

As in every war, those who suffered most were the innocents. Here a South Vietnamese boy takes care of his younger brother.

negotiation as an alternative to the war in South Vietnam.

Early in 1966, Westmoreland flew to Hawaii to discuss with Sharp the requirements of the spreading war in South Vietnam. Westmoreland thought the time was now ripe to begin his strategy's second phase, the active location and destruction of major communist formations in their sanctuary areas. He revealed that a strength of 439,000 men was needed, including 10,000 more from Asian allies whose forces were particularly important in the battle to win the "hearts and minds" of the South Vietnamese civilian population. The total requested by Westmoreland included not just combat troops, but large numbers of support troops in specialties such as signals, engineering, transportation, and aviation.

High-level Conference

At the last minute, the scope of this Hawaii conference was expanded. President Johnson decided to attend for a meeting with South Vietnam's government representatives, President Thieu and Premier Ky. Johnson also ordered the presence of Ambassador Lodge, Secretary of Defense McNamara, Secretary of State Dean Rusk, and the secretaries of agriculture, education, health, and welfare. This emphasized the

Marine, 1st Reconnaissance Battalion, U.S. Marine Corps, South Vietnam, 1966.

This man wears the "tiger stripe" utilities uniform with M1956 suspenders and combat pack, M1937 Browning Automatic Rifle belt, M1942 field dressing pouches, and Bata boots. His weapon is the light machine gun component of the Stoner 63 weapon system.

importance attached by the Americans to victory in the "hearts and minds" battle, the struggle to provide the South Vietnamese civilian population with the security to implement vital economic, political, and social developments as a way of reducing support for the Viet Cong.

At the conference, the South Vietnamese leaders pledged themselves to the twofold aims of defeating the communists on the battlefield and of creating in their country a new political and social order. The American and South Vietnamese leaders also discussed the way in which an objective assessment of the war's progress could be made. Unlike conventional wars, in which the movement of the front line can be used as a gauge, Vietnam lacked any real front lines, so another way to measure progress was needed. There was no simple solution, and the imponderable factors of the Vietnam War were generally measured in quantifiable factors such as percentages (how much of the civilian population was under government control and what proportion of the country's roads and waterways were open) and numbers (how many Viet Cong had been brought over to the government side, how many communist soldiers had been killed, and how many weapons had been captured). With hindsight, it is easy to see that this was an impossible task. The only factors that could really be assessed objectively were the numbers of communist dead and weapons captured. And there was often considerable dispute even with these two supposedly objective factors, especially about the body count of communist dead.

Steadily Widening Operational Arena

Westmoreland was trying to keep U.S. operations clear of South Vietnam's centers of population, but it was just not possible in 1966. These areas were the

The Viet Cong guerrillas were an elusive foe, who compensated for lack of heavy firepower by very high mobility in a campaign of attack and movement. U.S. forces had to respond at least partially with similar tactics, and extensive airmobile search-and-destroy operations were mounted in areas around the bases that could provide heavy artillery support as and when it was required.

very ones in which the Viet Cong sought to concentrate their strength and consolidate their hold as the N.V.A. built up its strength along the Cambodian and Laotian frontiers. This meant, for example, that the 1st Cavalry Division spent much of the year in the central coastal province on Binh Dinh, where it finally broke the control of a Viet Cong regiment that had long dominated the area.

The defense of Saigon was an A.R.V.N. responsibility, but Westmoreland was sufficiently concerned about the security of the South Vietnamese capital to locate U.S. forces on likely approach routes from the communist sanctuary areas, especially one that was only 30 miles away on the Cambodian frontier. In January 1966, the 1st Infantry Division, the 173rd Airborne Brigade, and an Australian battalion swept a large rubber plantation

once owned by the French tire company, Michelin, and then moved closer toward Saigon to repeat the process in the Boi Loi forest and Ho Bo wood areas of the notorious "Iron Triangle."

Operation in the "Iron Triangle"

Two brigades of the 25th Infantry Division undertook a similar sweep in Tay Ninh province northwest of Saigon on the frontier with Cambodia, while the division's other brigade operated in the central highlands. The latter experienced a number of firm contacts, and Westmoreland reinforced it with a brigade of the 101st Airborne Division and then the entire 1st Cavalry Division. The operation, typical of the war's diffuse combat operations, did have the

One of the ways in which the U.S. tried to counter the mobility and elusiveness of the Viet Cong was with a high volume of firepower from personal and squad weapons. These men carry a mass of small arms ammunition as well as machine gun belts and hand grenades, as they take part in a search-and-destroy operation by the 2nd Battalion, 35th Infantry Regiment, 3rd Brigade (Task Force), 25th Infantry Division, in June 1967.

desired effect of breaking up the communists' concentration and thereby removing any immediate threat of a communist offensive against the provincial capitals of the region.

Operation "Attleboro"

In the summer of 1966, the 199th Light Infantry Brigade arrived in South Vietnam, and Westmoreland deployed it on the edge of the communist sanctuary area known as War Zone C in Tay Ninh province. As the brigade probed into War Zone C, it became clear that the communists were in this instance prepared to stand and fight, so Lieutenant General Jonathan Seaman's I Field Force was reinforced by the 1st Infantry Division, 173rd Airborne Brigade, brigades from the 4th and 25th Infantry Divisions, and elements of an A.R.V.N. division for Operation "Attleboro," which involved 22,000 men. The largest operation of the war up to that time, it took place in the area northwest of the Michelin plantation and lasted from September 14 to November 24. The six weeks were characterized by hit-and-run fighting that cost the communists 2,130 dead before they fell back into Cambodia.

In the very north of South Vietnam, the area along the Demilitarized Zone was held by South Vietnamese formations. The two marine divisions of III Marine Amphibious Force were operating in the three provinces immediately to the south; they were to halt any North Vietnamese incursion across the Demilitarized Zone once it had been slowed by the A.R.V.N. forces. In February 1966, intelligence reports suggested that the North Vietnamese were about to depart from their previous infiltration route from Laos and Cambodia in favor of a direct advance south through the Demilitarized Zone. It was estimated that it would take the North Vietnamese several months to concentrate their force for this attack, so Westmoreland ordered the construction of two airfields close to the Demilitarized Zone. He also insisted that a port facility able to handle tank landing ships should be constructed at Hue, the former imperial city of Vietnam. These moves,

OPERATION ATTLEBORO: AND IRON TRIANGLE

the U.S. commander estimated, would allow the rapid flow of American reinforcements into the area if the situation became threatening.

Renewed Civil Disturbance

Part of the problem in the northern provinces of South Vietnam, which were the strongholds of the Buddhist faith, was a complete and continued opposition to the government of Thieu and Ky. According to the Buddhists, who

Operation "Attleboro" was a massive sweep by forces from three countries to clear hostile forces from the "Iron Triangle" and adjacent areas.

South Vietnam was a country that offered many aspects of idyllic perfection, but, as this photograph highlights, it was also a country torn by war. Attached to Mobile Support Team 2, this sailor keeps his M16A1 rifle handy as he watches the bank of the River Bassac in case he has to support members of a navy SEAL (Sea, Air, and Land) team conducting a sweep along the shoreline in November 1967.

had played a major part in the downfall of Diem, the new government had failed to make adequate provision for them in the new administration. Thus when the Saigon government removed General Nguyen Chanh Chi, a popular commander of I Tactical Corps Zone, the northern Buddhists saw an ideal opportunity for demonstrations designed to overthrow the administration of Diem and Ky. Rioting began in Da Nang and soon spread to Hue, and the Buddhists called on Buddhists in the A.R.V.N. to support them. On April 3, 3,000 men of the

A.R.V.N.'s 1st Division paraded through Hue to demand the replacement of Thieu and Ky. The demonstrators marched on the air base at Da Nang, and a pitched battle with the base's marine defenders was only just avoided.

As the threat of civil war in South Vietnam increased, the trouble soon spread to southern cities, including Saigon. Thieu and Ky had at first hoped to ride out the demonstrations, but the involvement of some A.R.V.N. units in the trouble made them determined to respond with force. Three South

Right: During Operation "Cedar Falls" in January 1967, men of the 2nd Battalion, 28th Infantry Regiment, 1st Infantry Division, uncovered a cache of communist weapons. Typically for the Viet Cong, they were an assortment of types in different calibers and from several countries. The weapons included Mauser rifles from Germany, sniper rifles from China, machine guns from China and the U.S.S.R., and American machine guns, submachine guns, rifles, and grenade launchers. The photograph shows a soldier with a flamethrower carefully examining the entrance to a Viet Cong underground tunnel complex.

Opposite Bottom: In areas where the communists were grouped in strength, had built up supply dumps, and had constructed extensive accommodation and command bunkers, heavy equipment such as this flamethrower tank proved their worth.

Left: An M88 VTR (Vehicle Tracked, Retriever) uses its bulldozer blade to create a dug-in position for an armored fighting vehicle during Operation "Cedar Falls" in January 1967.

Below: The 27th Infantry Regiment and Company "B," 85th Engineer Batallion, creates a block along the River Saigon, to isolate the Viet Cong-controlled village of Phu Hoa Dong.

U.S. infantrymen move forward to destroy the survivors of a Viet Cong unit that had been trapped by a search-and-destroy sweep as it attempted to overrun an American artillery position.

Men of the 173rd Engineer Company, 173rd Airborne Brigade, prepare the explosive charge to demolish a Viet Cong underground bunker complex during operation "Cedar Falls" in January 1967. The Viet Cong were extraordinarily accomplished in the construction of such complexes; they were often very large and contained, and in addition to hidden entrances and firing positions, had most of the facilities needed for long-term habitation.

Vietnamese marine battalions were sent to Da Nang on April 4 in a show of force intended to give the demonstrators pause for thought, and a tense lull followed. Colonel Arch Hamblen played the key role in preventing a clash between the armed units loyal to each side. Four more South Vietnamese battalions arrived in Da Nang on May 15, triggering off another bout of rioting that lasted until the middle of June, when a South Vietnamese airborne task force slowly began to restore order. This outbreak of religious fervor in the north proved to be the last bout of civil disturbance that would trouble South Vietnam.

Successful Elections

As part of their effort to quell the disturbances, Thieu and Ky had promised a new constitution and free elections. The elections went ahead, and despite in-

A Sikorsky CH-54A Tarhe flying-crane helicopter prepares to lift an airmobile firing platform, complete with its 105-mm (4·13-inch) howitzer, of Battery "C," 3rd Battalion, 34th Artillery Regiment, 9th Infantry Division.

A touch of home and tradition for a man of the 1st Battalion, 4th Marine Regiment, 3rd Marine Division, involved in Operation ''Kentucky V'' during December 1967.

timidation by the Viet Cong, they proved remarkably successful in creating a new constituent assembly. This initial election was followed in the spring of 1967 by hamlet and village elections. In September, senate and presidential elections were held, and finally in October lower house representatives were elected. The presidential elections returned Thieu as president and Ky as vice-president.

The failure of their efforts to interfere with these elections prompted the communists to make a greater armed effort in the north, and there was a noticeable increase in the number of N.V.A. soldiers infiltrating through the Demilitarized zone. Westmorland ordered Walt to tackle the problem directly, and after an initial marine battalion had run into the N.V.A.'s 324th Division, Walt committed another six marine battalions. The fighting in Quang Tri province lasted until the end of September, and the force of 8,000 marines and 3,000 A.R.V.N. soldiers killed some 2,000 communists and forced the N.V.A. division to fall back to a sanctuary in the Demilitarized Zone, which was officially bombed for the first time on July 30.

Westmoreland was still worried about the northern provinces, for part of the reason for the 324th Division's defeat was

Boeing Vertol CH-46A Sea Knight helicopters line the flight deck of the amphibious assault ship U.S.S. *Tripoli*. There was never any chance that an amphibious operation against North Vietnam might be executed, so such vessels and helicopters were used to support U.S. Marine Corps' formations fighting in South Vietnam.

that the American and A.R.V.N. force had caught it before it had been able to concentrate. The area of greatest concern was around Khe Sanh, an outpost in northwestern Quang Tri province that served as the base for units patroling into Laos and contained an airstrip for the forward air control aircraft that spotted for tactical warplanes striking at targets just inside Laos.

Khe Sanh was therefore important for current operations, and it had longer-term significance for two purposes. It was the jumping-off point for large-scale operations Westmoreland still hoped to launch against communist sanctuaries in Laos, and it was the western end of the chain of defensive positions running just south of the Demilitarized Zone.

Defense of the North

The only way in which to stop communist infiltration through the Demilitarized Zone was to create a defensive line from the Laotian frontier all the way to the sea, but this would merely force the communists to rely more heavily on the Ho Chi Minh Trail. Westmorland, however, lacked the manpower either to construct or to man such a defensive

Above: Men of the 1st Cavalry Division (Airmobile) herd Viet Cong prisoners toward the nearest American base. Captured in mountain caves, these prisoners would be interrogated and interned in a camp intended for the re-education of communists.

Left: Operation "Cook" was undertaken during October 1967 in the mountains of Quang Ngai province 320 miles northeast of Saigon. During the operation, men of the 2nd Battalion, 502nd Parachute Infantry Regiment, 101st Airborne Division, captured this Viet Cong guerrilla, who is being questioned with the aid of a south Vietnamese army interpreter.

Armed with a 7·62-mm (0·3-inch) caliber M14 rifle, this man of the 1st Battalion, 5th Marine Regiment, 1st Marine Division, was leader of a 7·62-mm caliber M60 machine gun team. As has been the case with soldiers in wars throughout history, he seized every moment possible during operations to relax and recover his energies, both physical and emotional.

position, so he had to plan a more feasible alternative. This emerged as a "strongpoint obstacle system," a series of fire-support bases designed to channel infiltrators into areas where the marines could annihilate them by deploying their mobile reserves, heavier artillery, and decisively superior air power. Late in 1966, the Americans began construction of the system, with four bases (including Khe Sanh) forward and three back.

Work was already well underway when McNamara told the U.S. press that the United States was planning to construct a barrier of combat bases linked by barbed wire, mines, and electronic sensors. The secretary of defense had been convinced by his over-optimistic scientific advisers that such a "McNamara Line" would halt infiltration past the Demilitarized Zone, but failed to appreciate that operation of the line would require considerable manpower: without supporting manpower, the line could be dismantled by the communists. Westmoreland pointed out this fact to McNamara and showed the secretary of defense that a linear defense system of this type was not only more costly, but also less effective than the kind

of defense in depth he was planning to channel infiltrators into killing zones. The "McNamara Line" was promptly forgotten, but the North Vietnamese responded to Westmoreland's scheme by bringing up long-range artillery that could fire over the Demilitarized Zone and make the construction of Westmoreland's combat bases far more complicated and lengthy than he had anticipated.

Increased Manpower

By the end of 1966, the United States had 385,000 men in South Vietnam. There were five infantry divisions, two marine divisions, four independent brigades, and one armored cavalry regiment with M48 battle tanks. The equivalent of three full corps, this force was supplemented by 329,000 A.R.V.N. soldiers and 300,000 in the militia force known as the Regional and Popular Forces. During the year, however, the North Vietnamese had introduced another 60,000 men (the equivalent of five divisions) into South Vietnam, raising the strength of the communist forces to an

The General Dynamics F-111A was the world's first operational warplane with variable-geometry wings, which could be swept between the minimum- and maximum-sweep positions: the former offered a short take-off run and long cruising range at modest speed, while the latter provided very high ''dash'' speed and the smoothest possible ride at low level. The type was evaluated in Vietnam before many of the development problems had been overcome and initially suffered a heavy loss rate. Once these difficulties had been overcome, the F-111A began to mature as an exceptional low-level interdictor with advanced electronics, including the terrain-following radar that allowed high-speed flight at very low level. The type was thus able to deliver large loads of weapons over considerable range with a very high degree of accuracy. Manned by two men seated side-by-side in a jettisonable escape capsule, the F-111A was powered by two 18,500-pound afterburning thrust Pratt & Whitney TF30-P-3 turbofans for a maximum take-off weight of 91,300 pounds and a maximum speed ranging between 1,650 miles per hour, (Mach 2·5) at high altitude, and 915 miles per hour, (Mach 1·2) at sea level. The type spanned 63 feet with the wings spread and 31 feet 11·4 inches with the wings swept. The armament was carried in a small, lower-fuselage weapons bay and on six swiveling hardpoints under the wings up to a maximum weight of 30,000 pounds, including a 20-mm six-barrel cannon in the forward part of the weapons bay.

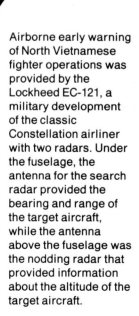

estimated 300,000 men. In these circumstances, Westmoreland felt that he needed another 100,000 men or more, and he urged that a reserve of three divisions should be created for despatch to South Vietnam as and when it was needed.

Westmoreland got the additional manpower he requested, but the Joint Chiefs of Staff turned down the idea of a three-division reserve unless the president called up reservists. Johnson refused, largely as a result of the social and political pressure beginning to mount against the U.S. involvement in South Vietnam. Much of this pressure was coming from academics and their students, and it was these unwilling students who would make up a vociferous percentage of an enlarged draft.

More Fighting Strength for the Communists

The beginning of 1967 was marked by a steady increase in North Vietnamese strength, including substantially larger quantities of artillery, within the Demilitarized Zone. Created by the Geneva Accords of 1954 and up to this time relatively untouched by either side, the zone was a natural area for the extension of communist control. Yet the State Department was unwilling to allow operations in the zone for fear of the propaganda capital that the communists would no doubt make of the fact. In the short term, therefore, the U.S. forces were allowed merely to return artillery fire from the zone; only in February 1967 were they allowed to undertake preemptive rather than retaliatory action with artillery and warplanes. It took longer still for Westmoreland to get permission for his ground forces to enter the zone, and even then they were restricted to pursuit of communist forces encountered south of the zone and were not allowed to pass the mid-point of the zone, roughly along the Ben Hai River.

The driving force in these decisions was the Department of State, which was extremely worried that any U.S. expansion of the war might draw China into the conflict. (After the war, it became clear that China had no intention of being

Airborne early warning of North Vietnamese fighter operations was provided by the Lockheed EC-121, a military development of the classic Constellation airliner with two radars. Under the fuselage, the antenna for the search radar provided the bearing and range of the target aircraft, while the antenna above the fuselage was the nodding radar that provided information about the altitude of the target aircraft.

1966 had been a year of American preparation. In 1967, the Americans would make major efforts to win the war.

By 1967 our base development was nearing completion, our in-country logistics system was established, and our forces build up was nearing completion. We were ready to seize the initiative throughout most of South Vietnam, thereby applying continuous pressure on the enemy. Our military objectives were always related to the security of population. Therefore, we sought to frustrate the enemy's plans and drive his main forces well away from the populated areas so as to destroy them in the hinterland and to open the roads to allow pacification to proceed. We would block and defeat his attacks when they occurred, and follow up by exploitation and pursuit allowing him no victories on the battlefield. Our increased air and naval power would be exploited to maximum advantage. Vietnamese forces were to concentrate their primary efforts on the support of Revolutionary Development activities, defense of population and governmental centers, and protection and control of national resources, particularly rice and salt. In support of these operations, our advisory effort would continue to emphasize the development of the Vietnamese military forces and to encourage their support of the government's Revolutionary Development program.
Strategically the major emphasis would be placed on securing the III Corps area around Saigon, which contained a substantial part of the population and commerce of the Republic.

Operation Cedar Falls was the first large-scale offensive conducted by American forces. The target was a Viet Cong-dominated area some 20 miles northwest of Saigon.

In the early morning hours, January 8 (1967), people in Ben Sue Village went calmly about their tasks. At exactly 8 a.m., total confusion erupted. The once-clear sky filled with 60 helicopters. The choppers swooped in, allowing division soldiers to unload and begin to seal off the village. Minutes later the sky was filled again as the aircraft vanished as quickly as they had appeared.

Flying a gunship, Major Goerge B. Fish, from the 1st Aviation Battalion, zoomed over the trees to mark three key landing zones while the main flight was one minute out. His crew chief recalled,

"We were flying in one area when I heard over the radio 'Rebel 36, go in for the mark.' We went in at low level at about eighty-five miles an hour. We received fire from a bunker and returned it. . . . It didn't fire anymore. . . . And you look out to see a whole bunch of choppers . . . you see a fantastic mess . . . beautifully coordinated and planned."

Major Donald A. Ice, the commander of A Company, led his flight over the jungle and along the river to a landing zone in the northeast corner of Ben Suc.

"As we flew along the river our skids were almost in the water," he recalled. *"Then we jumped a treeline, flared up and popped into the landing zone. I had to push Vietnamese out of the zone. They didn't know what was happening."*

The choppers touched down simultaneously in landing zones to the west, north, and east of the town while the "Eagle Flight" guarded the south. In less than one and one-half minutes an entire infantry battalion, some 420 men, was on the ground. . . .
Just after the assault ships had departed, helicopters with loudspeakers and South Vietnamese Army announcers aboard circled the village at low altitude and broadcast the following message:
"Attention the people of Ben Suc. You are surrounded by the Republic of South Vietnam and allied forces. Do not run away or you will be shot as VC. Stay in your homes and wait for further instructions."
The inhabitants were then further instructed to go immediately to the old schoolhouse.
Most of the villagers followed the instructions; those who attempted to evade and leave the village were engaged by the blocking forces. Adjacent rivers were patrolled for any escapees. Tactical surprise was almost complete; the enemy was unable to offer any cohesive resistance to the landing. . . .
Company A, 1st Battalion, 26th Infantry, was one of the first units on the ground and

quickly formed up after clearing its landing zone. As the point squad moved forward from the landing zone towards its designated blocking position, tragedy struck. Two command-detonated claymore mines exploded and two men fell. A large booby trap mounted in a tree exploded and its fragments downed two more men. The squad had wandered into an enemy minefield. Staff Sergeant Ernest Williams of San Francisco, California, rushed forward to set up security for the wounded and to get them medical aid. The platoon medical corpsman was injured when he stepped on an antipersonnel mine while trying to aid the wounded. Specialist Four Astor Rogers of Chicago, Illinois, another medic, hurried forward. When enemy sniper fire began coming in on his position, Sergeant Williams brought his men on line and laid down a base of fire in coordination with his platoon leader. "Through enemy fire and a heavy mine field these men functioned with total disregard for their own lives and safety," said Captain Rudolf Egersdorfer, Company A commander. "They are a credit to the unit.". . .

It was to be expected that uprooting the natives of these villages would evoke resentment, and it did. They had lived under and with the Viet Cong and had supported them for the past three years; nor was it easy for the natives to give up their homes and the land they had been working. The villagers were permitted to take with them anything they could carry, pull, or herd, to include their water buffalo. What they could not take was retrieved by the U.S. and South Vietnamese troops and returned to the natives at the relocation center. A total of 5,987 persons was evacuated (582 men, 1,651 women, and 3,754 children). Also moved to the relocation site were 247 water buffalo, 225 head of cattle, 158 oxcarts, and 60 tons of rice.

At one point in the evacuation, a sow became separated from her twelve pigs as they where being loaded on one of the giant Chinook helicopters. She loudly made her loss known. General DePuy, who happened to stop by the loading site and learned of the mishap, instructed: "I want that sow reunited with her pigs before nightfall" Before long the sow was on her way to the relocation camp. . . .

As the villagers and their belongings moved out, bulldozers, tankdozers, and demolition teams moved in. Since Ben Suc was not yet totally deserted, the initial dozers set about clearing a scrub jungle area in the southwest corner of the village known by the troops as the briar patch. As Colonel Kiernan, commanding officer of the 1st Engineer Battalion, recalled:
. . . .I guess it was about twenty acres of scrub jungle. . . . The place was so infested with tunnels that as my dozers would knock over the stumps of trees, the VC would pop out from behind the dozers. We captured about . . . six or eight VC one morning. They just popped out of the tunnels and we picked them up. . . . After the civilians were taken from the town, we went through and methodically knocked down the homes . . . tunnels were throughout the whole area. . . .

The bulldozers moved through the former Viet Cong stronghold and razed the structures to the ground, crushing ruins, collapsing tunnels, and obliterating bunkers and underground storage rooms. When the village had been flattened by the engineers, there was yet one more blow to be dealt to Ben Suc by Colonel Kiernan's professionals. A large cavity was scooped out near the center of the area, filled with ten thousand pounds of explosives – many no longer usable in normal operations, covered, tamped, and then set off by a chemical fuze within minutes of the predicted time of detonation. The hope was that the blast might crush any undiscovered tunnels in the village.

One of the major objectives of Operation Cedar Falls had been achieved; the village of Ben Suc no longer existed.

In spite of this effort, the Viet Cong soon returned to the Iron Triangle. From its hidden camps and tunnels, they staged the decisive Tet Offensive against Saigon one year later.

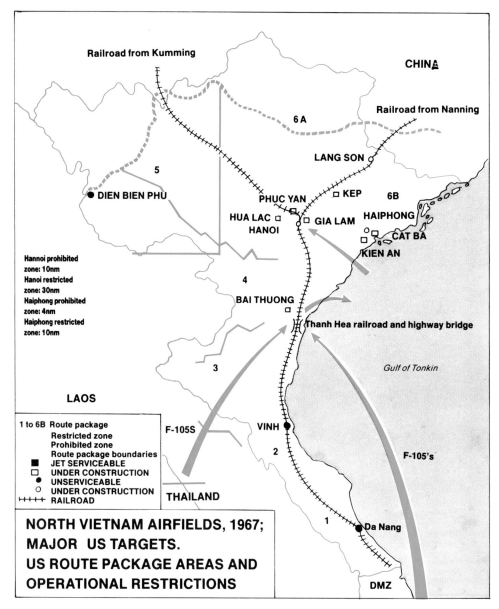

U.S. bomber sectors
and major targets in
North Vietnam.

Railroad from Kumming

CHINA

6 A

Railroad from Nanning

LANG SON

5

KEP

6B

DIEN BIEN PHU

PHUC YAN

HUA LAC

GIA LAM

HAIPHONG

HANOI

CAT BA

KIEN AN

Hannoi prohibited
zone: 10nm
Hanoi restricted
zone: 30nm
Haiphong prohibited
zone: 4nm
Haiphong restricted
zone: 10nm

4

BAI THUONG

Thanh Hea railroad and highway bridge

3

Gulf of Tonkin

LAOS

1 to 6B Route package
        Restricted zone
        Prohibited zone
        Route package boundaries
■   JET SERVICEABLE
□   UNDER CONSTRUCTION
●   UNSERVICEABLE
○   UNDER CONSTRUCTTION
++++ RAILROAD

F-105S

VINH

2

F-105's

THAILAND

**NORTH VIETNAM AIRFIELDS, 1967;
MAJOR US TARGETS.
US ROUTE PACKAGE AREAS AND
OPERATIONAL RESTRICTIONS**

1

Da Nang

DMZ

The terrain and
climate were often as
much the enemy as the
communists, as this
unhappy marine found
during Operation
"Deckhouse VI" in
February 1967.

drawn into a direct role. Although North Vietnam made frequent appeals for help from other communist countries, it was wholly unprepared to take any of the advice that always accompanied such aid.)

The Threat to Khe Sanh

Westmoreland remained sure that a major North Vietnamese offensive was imminent in the north. He strengthened III Marine Amphibious Force with two battalions of long-range 175-mm (6·89-inch) guns. In addition, he ordered the construction of a new airfield near the city of Quang Tri, upgraded Khe Sanh's airstrip, and allocated priority for B-52 tactical attacks to the force. As a contingency move, Westmoreland instructed his chief of staff, Major General William B. Rosson, to form the headquarters of "Task Force Oregon" that would take three independent infantry brigades under command to become the 23rd (Americal) Division for the defense of the southern part of I Tactical Corp Zone and so free III Marine Amphibious Force for operations in the north.

By March 1967, the North Vietnamese were ready to attack. On March 20, a barrage of more than 1,000 artillery rounds was fired against the fire-support bases at Con Thien and Gio Linh. A marine supply convoy was ambushed, and patrols from the forward fire-support bases ran into strong North Vietnamese opposition. On March 24, a marine patrol from Khe Sanh ran into a considerably larger N.V.A. force, which set off the "hill fights" for Hills 861, 881 North, and 881 South. (The numerals referred to the hills' heights in meters.) The hills had been occupied by an N.V.A. division as the first step in a major effort planned against the fire-support base at Khe Sanh. Supported by tactical warplanes and 175-mm artillery fire, the marines fought their way up the three hills in some of the hardest fighting of the Vietnam War, drove off the North Vietnamese, and established forward positions of their own to protect Khe

Sanh. This eased the immediate pressure on Khe Sanh; the N.V.A. switched its attentions to the fire-support base at Con Thien. Extremely heavy concentrations of North Vietnamese artillery fire fell on the base and its protective features, but the gathering of N.V.A. units for the planned assault was badly delayed by offensive sweeps made by marines with the type of accurate support from artillery and tactical warplanes that was increasingly a feature of American combat operations.

An American Dien Bien Phu?

Parts of the increasingly unsympathetic American press began to report Con Thien as an "American Dien Bien Phu," a piece of useless ground whose defense offered no real tactical advantage but which would consume many American lives. This was categorically denied by Westmoreland and Lieutenant General Robert E. Cushman, Jr., who succeeded Walt on June 1. The two commanders were sure that Con Thien could be held not with American lives but with American firepower, and that the base was tactically important: if the Americans abandoned it and fell back to the next line of bases, the N.V.A. would merely move forward to this line, and in the process come closer to their objective of taking the two northernmost provinces of South Vietnam.

As the fighting continued, the Americans responded with increasingly heavy support firepower directed from a forward headquarters established by Lieutenant General William M. Momyer, commander of the 7th Air Force. This firepower included both air force and marine warplanes, B-52 heavy bombers, and naval gunfire cooperating with land-based artillery. There is little doubt that this firepower played a decisive role in preventing the N.V.A. from building up the concentration of manpower that might have allowed them to overrun Con Thien. In the fall of 1967, the fighting for Con Thien withered away as the communists pulled back and began to plan their

Operation "Fairfax"

During this period, there had been a steady flow of American troops into South Vietnam. This additional strength at last permitted Westmoreland to undertake some of the operations he had long thought necessary. Some of them lasted for months rather than weeks. Typical was Operation "Fairfax," which took place in the dense clustering of villages around Saigon and involved a U.S. brigade and a group of South Vietnamese rangers. Working mainly at night, the Americans and South Vietnamese concentrated their efforts on saturation patrols and ambushes designed to prevent the Viet Cong from moving freely among the civilian population to extract "taxes,"

gather supplies, and recruit. It was very hard to quantify the results of such operations, which were also undertaken in Binh Dinh province and the Rung Sat. In Binh Dinh province, the communists had earlier been driven out, but now strong Viet Cong forces returned, supported by an N.V.A. regiment, and were again challenged by the 1st Cavalry Division. The Rung Sat is a region of mangrove swamps at the mouth of the Saigon River, and its inhospitable nature meant that Americans operating there were rotated on a daily basis to prevent their infection with a number of diseases and conditions such as "immersion foot."

Operation "Cedar Falls"

Other operations were more conventional

Operation "Fairfax," a search-and-destroy sweep undertaken around Saigon during May 1967, involved the 199th Light Infantry Brigade. Here dog handlers and their animals of the 49th Scout Dog Platoon search a house in the village of Long Trung, 5 miles northeast of Saigon.

Left: A U.S. Air Force Lockheed C-130 Hercules transport airplane blazes fiercely at Da Nang Air Base in July 1967 after a Viet Cong rocket had impacted close to it.

Above: A member of Company A, 4th Battalion, 12th infantry climbs a muddy bank after completing a search and seizure mission in the village of Long Trung during Operation ''Fairfax.''

in the purely military sense, and they took longer to organize. Typical was Operation "Cedar Falls," involving 15,000 men of three divisions (one of them South Vietnamese), an airborne brigade, and an armored cavalry regiment. The operational area was the "Iron Triangle," a 60-square-mile area of forest interspersed by rice paddies and villages, about 20 miles up the Saigon River from the South Vietnamese capital. The "Iron Triangle" had long been a communist sanctuary and base for terrorist activities in Saigon.

On January 8, 1967, the operation began with the heliborne landing of an allied detachment in the village of Ben Suc, which intelligence claimed was the center of the communist defense network in the area. To make sure that the operation achieved complete surprise, the Americans had not informed the South Vietnamese and thereby avoided the possibility of a "leak" by a communist sympathizer. The other side of the coin, however, was that a considerable refugee problem developed as soon as the operation started. The administration of Binh Duong province was overwhelmed, and it was several days before shelter and

Watching cautiously for any indication of a Viet Cong ambush, men of the 199th Light Infantry Brigade move out after searching a South Vietnamese village in Operation "Fairfax."

food could be arranged. The refugees' dismal conditions were a natural target for U.S. newsmen, who filed many condemnatory reports.

As the initial air-mobile landing took place, the other forces involved in the operation surrounded the "Iron Triangle." As usual, the numbers of men available were too small, and the cordon around the sanctuary area was therefore too loose. By the end of the operation on January 26, only some 750 communists had been killed. But 280 prisoners had been captured, 540 people had defected from the communist cause, 512 suspected communists were detained, and a considerable quantity of small arms, ammunition, and other materiel had been captured.

The operation's overall objective was the elimination of the "Iron Triangle" as a communist sanctuary, which also meant the removal and relocation of almost 6,000 civilians so that their villages in the "Iron Triangle" could be destroyed. The military would ideally have liked to level the whole area, but lacked the equipment for such a task. So they restricted themselves to cutting wide swathes through the forest so that communist movements could be detected more easily as they crossed the cleared section amounting to 4¼ square miles (11 sq km). The communists returned in strength within a week of the operation's end, however, but the "Iron Triangle" was now a "free-fire zone" into which heavy artillery could fire at will. Eventually, special bulldozers called Rome plows were used to level the entire area, and it ceased to be a useful sanctuary for the communists.

American casualties in "Cedar Falls" were 72 killed and 37 wounded, and materiel losses were light.

Operation "Junction City"

Another undertaking of the same type was Operation "Junction City" between February 22 and May 14, 1967. It involved more than 25,000 American and South Vietnamese troops, and was designed to clear the communists out of War Zone C in Tay Ninh province along the frontier with Cambodia. It was also intended to

Above: During a firefight with Viet Cong guerrillas in Operation "Junction City," undertaken in February 1967, a man of the 2nd Battalion, 27th Infantry Regiment, 2nd Brigade, 25th Infantry Division, moves to a better position. A companion waits nearby, ready to provide covering fire with his M16 automatic rifle, which has a 40-mm grenade launcher under its barrel.

Below: Men of the 2nd Battalion, 27th Infantry Regiment, guard Viet Cong supplies captured in Operation "Junction City."

OPERATION 'JUNCTION CITY'

22 Feb-17 March 1967
Communist HQ forced to
withdraw into Cambodia

Left: Operation ''Junction City'' could not prevent large numbers of communist troops from escaping into Cambodia.

Below: Operation ''Pershing'' was a search-and-destroy mission undertaken by the 1st Battalion, 7th Cavalry Regiment, 1st Cavalry Division (Airmobile), during July 1967 in the An Lao valley of Binh Dinh province. Here an M55 0·5-inch (12·7-mm) quadruple heavy machine-gun mounting of an attached artillery unit fires across the mouth of the valley to discourage any communist attempts to filter out of the area.

capture, if possible, the headquarters of the Central Office for South Vietnam, the organization established by the North Vietnamese communist party for the political control of South Vietnam.

The American and South Vietnamese forces were concentrated in a large loop around the three sides of War Zone C in South Vietnam and began to drive into the communist sanctuary. The operation also saw the only parachute jump of the Vietnam War, when a battalion of the 173rd Airborne Brigade jumped into the open end of the sanctuary at Katum. Yet the escape route to Cambodia could not be closed, and most of the communist troops, together with the staff from the headquarters of the COSVN, evaded the

American and South Vietnamese forces to reach this haven.

The communists lost 2,728 killed and 34 taken prisoner, and another 139 defected in response to the 9.77 million leaflets that were dropped to supplement the 102 hours of aerial loudspeaker appeals. Another 65 people were detained as suspected communists. Other gains for the Americans and South Vietnamese were the capture of much *materiel*, supplies, and more than 500,000 pages of documents, and the destruction of 5,000 or more bunkers and other military structures.

American casualties were 282 men killed and another 1,576 wounded, while materiel included three tanks,

Previous Page Top:
Men of the 9th Cavalry Regiment, 1st Cavalry Division (Airmobile), await orders during Operation ''Pershing.'' The task of the lead (or point) soldier was to check the ground before the rest of his party entered it.

Previous Page Bottom:
Still clutching his rifle and wearing camouflage, a junior officer of the U.S. Navy's SEAL Team One keeps a watchful eye on the passing jungle. His team has been picked up by a navy landing craft after a sweep along the bank of the River Bassac.

Keeping a tight hold on his M1 carbine, a man of the South Vietnamese National Police questions an old man, believed to be a Viet Cong sympathizer, in a village searched during Operation ''Pershing.''

Marines load a casualty onto a Sikorsky UH-34E helicopter for evacuation to a hospital as they continue their search-and-destroy mission.

Men of the 1st Cavalry Division (Airmobile) involved in Operation "Pershing" take cover on the edge of a dry paddy field as friendly artillery fire bursts on a mountainside thought to contain a Viet Cong bunker complex. The location was near Base Camp English, 40 miles northeast of An Khe.

Men of the 3rd Battalion, 60th Infantry Regiment, 9th Infantry Division, wade through the treacherous waters of the "Killer Swamp" area in August 1967 as part of Operation "Coronado."

Men of the 60th Infantry Regiment thankfully board a navy landing craft after completing their sweep through the "Killer Swamp" in Operation "Coronado."

A marine 81-mm (3·2-inch) mortar crew in action near Con Thien in October 1967.

In parallel with the outright military program, a large but often misguided and generally unsuccessful effort was made to win the "hearts and minds" of the Vietnamese people. Here an American soldier sets up a film projector on top of his vehicle for the showing of a propaganda or public service film.

A hut in a Viet Cong village near Tan Dinh Island in the River Bassac burns after being hit by fire from a naval patrol boat in Operation ''Plaques Nine'' in November 1967.

These marines are on patrol in typical country southwest of Con Thien during Operation ''Lancaster'' in November 1967.

21 armored personnel carriers, 12 trucks, four helicopters, five howitzers and two quadruple 0.5-inch machine gun mountings destroyed.

Continued operations were showing how difficult it was to trap the communists in any area, let alone those that bordered neutral territory where U.S. forces could not enter.

Americans Enter the Southern Zone

As these and similar operations proceeded, Westmoreland decided that the time was ripe for American forces to take a more active part in the IV Corps Tactical Zone. Located in the extreme

ASPBs (Assault Support Patrol Boats) of the U.S. Navy's Task Force 117 patrol a canal in the delta of the Mekong River as part of Operation "Coronado Nine" in December 1967. The ASPB was the only naval type specifically built for riverine warfare; at a displacement of 38 tons, it could reach 14 knots on its two 440-horsepower diesel engines, which were silenced so that stealthy operations could be undertaken. Among this boat's weapons are twin 0·5-inch (12·7-mm) heavy machine guns in the bow turret, a single 20-mm cannon in the turret above the conning position, and a single 20-mm cannon in an open mounting on the after deck.

A CCB (Command and Communications Boat) of Task Force 117 passes close to the river bank during Operation "Coronado Nine." Each task force had a normal complement of 52 ATCS (Armored Troop Carriers), five CCBs, 10 Monitors, and two ATC refueling craft, and were generally assigned 32 ASPBs.

south of South Vietnam. It was the country's most densely populated area and had hitherto been the responsibility of the South Vietnamese forces. The authorities had made this decision based on a fear that the general xenophobia of the ethnic South Vietnamese might be stronger in this more populous region than in other ethnic minority areas where American troops otherwise operated. But an American battalion had operated successfully in Long An province near Saigon, an area of comparable ethnic composition and density to the southern region, without raising the emotional temperature of the region unduly. The presence of American forces among them

seemed in fact to bolster the morale of South Vietnamese units, and the civilian population seemed to respond equally well to the work of American agencies in improving medical and dental facilities, building schools, digging wells, and improving bridges. Westmoreland therefore decided that U.S. forces could be used closer to the ethnic South Vietnamese population.

The plan called now for a U.S. division to become part of the forces in IV Corps Tactical Zone. Of the division's three brigades, two would serve in their standard ground role, while the third would cooperate with a U.S. Navy force of accommodation ships, artillery platform barges, troop transports, minesweepers, and the type of armored gunboats known as monitors. The navy and army personnel of this Riverine Force would operate against the communists in the extraordinary complex of rivers and canals that veined South Vietnam's southern provinces.

The Riverine Force

The creation of a base for the Riverine Force in the delta of the Mekong River was a considerable technical feat, lasting for about two years. The required basin was created by excavating many rice paddies, and the dirt was combined with dredged mud to create an artificial island one mile square. The work was attacked by the communists on occasion, and three dredgers were sunk. Operations in this watery communist haven were started even before the base had been completed, but meant that the men, like those operating in the Rung Sat, had to be rotated back to the accommodation ships at frequent intervals to "dry out."

One of the consequences of the

The aircraft carrier U.S.S. *Forrestal* approaches Mayport, Florida, in August 1967. About two weeks earlier, on July 29, an accident had started a series of fires and explosions on the carrier's flight deck as the ship patroled in the Gulf of Tonkin: before the situation had been brought under control in an 18-hour fight, 134 men had been killed and 21 aircraft destroyed. Evidence of the fire can be seen all over the aft section of the flight deck and on the stern.

Above Left: A man from one of the LRRP (Long-Range Reconnaissance Patrol) team of the 1st Cavalry Division (Airmobile) prepares his meal during Operation ''Jeb Stuart III'' in the National Forest Reserve south of Quang Tri in August 1968.

Above Right: Men of the 1st Cavalry Division (Airmobile) move with difficulty down a hillside whose forest had earlier been destroyed by artillery fire or aerial bombardment.

Left: A Boeing Vertol CH-47A Chinook twin-rotor helicopter delivers a water trailer to men of the 3rd Battalion, 12th Infantry Regiment, 4th Infantry Division, at a base camp in the central highlands during September 1967.

Carrying a large load of personal gear as well as a personal weapon and, in the case of the man on the right, an antitank rocket launcher, soldiers of the 1st Battalion, 8th Infantry Regiment, 4th Infantry Division, pause to fill their canteens in a mountain stream during Operation "MacArthur" in the highland region around Dak To in November 1967.

comparatively small American commitment was the frequent relocation of forces from one area to another as the perceived communist threat shifted. As was pointed out even at the time, this meant that the Americans were not able to win the trust of the local population as effectively as they might otherwise have been able to do. The reason was simple: the local population was unwilling to commit itself to the Americans, who might then move on, leaving them to the less capable protection of the South Vietnamese forces and the greater wrath of the returning communists.

There seemed to be no alternative to this system, so the defense of the civilian population rested with the A.R.V.N. and with the Regional and Popular Forces. The latter had to play a full part in the defense of South Vietnam despite its low fighting skills; and in platoon- and company-sized packets, it generally manned the small triangular forts of baked mud bricks located on the edge of many villages and hamlets. With these forces screening them from the worst excesses of the communists, the civilian population of South Vietnam underwent the pacifica-

tion process designed to improve local government, to identify, finance, and aid self-help projects, and to locate and eliminate communist cadres. The South Vietnamese and American civil agencies, supported by South Vietnamese and American intelligence agencies, seemed to be making adequate rather than startling progress in this program during 1967. Even so, the Johnson administration came under increasingly hostile opposition from the American media and people during this period.

Heavier Casualties

Part of the problem was that, despite encouraging official reports, no end to the war seemed to be in sight. Large numbers of U.S. media personnel were in South Vietnam, and they were filing damning reports accompanied by color film of the war and its brutal effects on civilians as well as soldiers. At the same time, the American casualty roll was growing and was threatening to overtake the list for the Korean War. Between 1961 and 1965, American casualties in South Vietnam totaled 1,484 dead and 7,337 wounded; in 1966, the commitment of U.S. forces to a combat role in Vietnam resulted in the deaths of 5,047 American military personnel.

Johnson thought that a good way to strike back at the growing opposition would be a public statement of American aims and successes by Westmoreland. The general returned to the United States to speak at an Associated Press dinner in April 1967. The occasion was disastrous, for the media took great exception to Westmoreland's assertion that criticism of the American effort aided the enemy and cost American lives, while the then small but energetic anti-war movement was angered by the general's condemnation of people who burned the American flag and by his claim that "through a clever combination of psychological and political warfare," the enemy had won wide public support "which gives him hope that he can win politically that which he cannot accomplish militarily."

"Minimum Essential Force" or "Optimum Force"?

Shortly afterward, Westmoreland attended a White House conference of

An M113 armored personnel carrier of Troop "A," 1st Squadron, 1st Cavalry Regiment, Americal Division, breasts a ridge during a sweep in August 1968. Such vehicles were proof against most weapons carried by the Viet Cong, but were vulnerable to mines, in whose use the enemy became highly skilled.

Above Left: Men of the 8th Infantry Regiment, 4th Infantry Division, move along the bank of a mountain stream during Operation ''MacArthur.''

Above Right: A marine mortar crew fires 60-mm (2·36-inch) bombs at North Vietnamese troops trying to escape from a valley attacked in Operation ''Essex'' during November 1967.

Left: A Sikorsky UH-34 helicopter brings in reinforcements and supplies for marines during an October 1967 operation.

political and military leaders. Based on the level of success achieved by the eight American divisions he already had in South Vietnam, Westmoreland had already submitted two proposals to the president. One involved what Westmoreland called the ''minimum essential force'' of 550,000 men, and the other what he called the ''optimum force'' of 670,000 men. Though he was unwilling to commit himself, Westmoreland reluctantly agreed at the conference that with the ''minimum essential force'' he could end the American commitment to the war in about five years, and with the ''optimum force'' in about three years.

Johnson discussed the options at great length with McNamara and other senior figures in his administration. The president wanted to force the North Vietnamese to the negotiating table before the presidential elections of November 1968, but this problem was made more difficult by the fact that there was clearly no sure way of ending the war without invading North Vietnam, Laos, or Cambodia, and risking the intervention of the Chinese with all the attendant dangers of a major war. As he intended to run again, Johnson had to make careful consideration of factors such as the effect that calling up the reserves would have on the growingly vociferous anti-war faction, and the result that putting the country on a higher war footing would have on the federal social programs associated with his "Great Society" concept. In July 1967, therefore, Johnson decided that Westmoreland could have only another 47,000 men, raising the U.S. strength in South Vietnam to 525,000, 25,000 less than the "minimum essential force."

Whatever Johnson had hoped, this did nothing to appease the anti-war faction, which used high-profile personalities such as movie stars, novelists, and even a celebrated pediatrician to pontificate on foreign policy matters and put the anti-war message over to the American public.

Official reports from Saigon and a personal meeting with Ellsworth Bunker, the new American ambassador in South Vietnam, convinced Johnson that real progress was being made in the struggle against the communists. Yet he was shaken by the increasingly vocal opposition to the war, and in November 1967 Bunker and Westmoreland went to Washington, where they again assured the American public that the war was being won. The most important of these assurances came on December 21, when Westmoreland told a television audience that "We have reached an important point when the end begins to come into view." Westmoreland went on to say that the war was reaching the point at which the burden could be transferred increasingly to the South Vietnamese forces, whose progressive improvement

A Lockheed C-130 Hercules of the U.S. Marine Corps' air arm burns on the airstrip at Khe Sanh base camp in 1968. Eight people were killed and two survived after the plane was hit by small arms fire in the air and then by a mortar bomb after it touched down.

was the primary task of General Creighton W. Abrams, his second in command. Westmoreland concluded by making the bold assertion that within two years or less, token withdrawals of U.S. forces could begin.

Another Communist Offensive

While he was still in Washington, Westmoreland learned that heavy fighting had broken out in Kontum province of the central highlands. Communist forces, including one N.V.A. division, were attacking a frontier outpost manned by Montagnard tribesmen and men of the Special Forces. The third of the ''border battles'' fought in the fall of 1967, the attack was apparently a North Vietnamese effort to cause trouble during the period that Thieu and Ky were to be inaugurated as president and vice-president of South Vietnam.

With an escorting destroyer in the background, a Douglas A-1 Skyraider attack warplane prepares to touch down on the aircraft carrier U.S.S. *Coral Sea* after an attack on a target in North Vietnam during January 1968.

The first battle took place at Song Be, a village of Phuoc Long province, where an N.V.A. regiment that attacked the head-quarters of an A.R.V.N. battalion was driven back with heavy losses. The second battle was fought at Loc Ninh, a village of Binh Long province close to the South Vietnamese frontier with Cambodia. Here, Viet Cong and North Vietnamese regulars attacked a militia outpost, which was rapidly reinforced by elements of an A.R.V.N. division and a heliborne detachment of the 1st Cavalry Division. Although the fighting between October 29 and November 2 was very heavy, it resulted in another communist defeat. Despite "human wave" attacks, the communists could not take the post and lost some 900 men to the allies' 60.

In Washington, Westmoreland said that the American effort was hurting the communists badly, as reflected in a ten-to-one "kill ratio" in favor of the Americans during their own operations, and a still higher ratio in favor of the Americans when targets were more plentiful during communist operations. This, according to the general, suggested that the communists would be forced into a "momentous decision," in other words, a total reassessment of their overall strategy for South Vietnam.

By the time Westmoreland returned to South Vietnam, intelligence assessments of the "border battles" began to reveal that Westmoreland had probably been right in his basic conclusion, and that the battles were more than just an attempt to embarrass the South Vietnamese government. Just before the battle at Dak To, a captured North Vietnamese document revealed that the battle was in fact the preface to a major North Vietnamese offensive in Kontum province, a "concentrated offensive effort in coordination with other units in various battle areas throughout South Vietnam," including a "prolonged battle."

Heavy Fighting in the Central Highlands

The fighting around Dak To, the heaviest in the central highlands since the Ia Drang battle, eventually involved 16 U.S. bat-

A PACV (Patrol Air-Cushion Vehicle) of the U.S. Navy moves off for a sweep through the delta of the Mekong River.

talions. The North Vietnamese were eventually defeated, suffering some 1,400 dead as well as an unknown number wounded in the process. As the fighting around Dak To subsided, the marines patrolling the area around Khe Sanh began to detect signs of a North Vietnamese buildup in this area. Throughout the whole of South Vietnam, there were a large number of small but very vicious battles, and the number of people defecting from the communist cause declined rapidly. As Christmas approached, allied intelligence reported that North Vietnamese truck traffic on the Ho Chi Minh Trail in Laos had trebled.

Westmoreland reported to Washington and informed the Joint Chiefs of Staff that the communists had "already made a crucial decision concerning the conduct of the war" and that "prolongation of [their] past policies for conducting the war would lead to [their] defeat, and that [they] would have to make a major effort to reverse the downward trend." Westmoreland concluded that the communists were planning "to make a maximum effort on all fronts (political and military) in order to achieve victory in a short period of time."

Increasingly Worrying Evidence

From the beginning of January 1968, evidence continued to mount that the communists were indeed in the last stages of preparing a major effort. Around Khe Sanh, at least two N.V.A. divisions were concentrating, and a defecting communist officer reported that an all-out attack on Khe Sanh was to be made during the Tet holiday. Further indication of the communists' intentions was provided by a captured document, which stated that the time was nearly ripe for a "general offensive and general uprising [of the South Vietnamese people] to take over towns and cities [and] liberate Saigon." Another captured document covered a communist scheme for an offensive in Pleiku province before the Tet holiday.

Lieutenant General Fred C. Weyand, commanding II Field Force, came to the conclusion that the communist forces in

Men of the U.S. Marine Corps move a wounded comrade to a helicopter for evacuation to the hospital in Da Nang, just 15 miles to the northeast, during Operation "Worth" in 1968.

Soldiers of the 2nd Battalion, 16th Infantry Regiment, 1st Infantry Division, check wagons for concealed weapons and ammunition. Such tasks were often reserved for men who had been sent back to a major staging camp before going on R&R (Rest and Rehabilitation).

the III Corps Tactical Zone were shifting out of their sanctuary areas along the frontier with Cambodia toward Saigon. In Qui Nhon, on the central part of South Vietnam's eastern coast, 11 Viet Cong were captured in a house raided by A.R.V.N. troops, who also seized a tape recorder and two tapes. Under interrogation, the captured men revealed that Qui Nhon and other cities were to be attacked during the Tet holiday. The tapes contained propaganda material, and the prisoners confirmed that their task had been to broadcast the tapes as soon as the government radio station had been captured.

Major General Phillip B. Davidson, senior intelligence officer of the Military Assistance Command, Vietnam, cancelled all leave for U.S. forces and warned Westmoreland that major attacks could be expected right through South Vietnam, though the exact places and dates were not yet certain.

The Signs Point to Tet, 1968

On January 20, Westmoreland reported to the Joint Chiefs of Staff that "the enemy is presently developing a threatening posture in several areas in order to seek victories essential to achieving prestige and bargaining power. He may exercise his initiatives prior to, during, or after Tet." So seriously did Westmoreland take the threat that he persuaded Thieu to cancel the Tet ceasefire in the northern provinces and limit it to 24 hours in other areas.

As he could not predict the exact location and timing of the attacks, Westmoreland decided not to alert the media and via them the American people. The closest the general came to a public warning was a statement during a television interview that the communists were intending to launch "a major effort to win a spectacular battlefield success along the eve of Tet." Weyand also told a reporter that the communists were planning "critical – perhaps spectacular – moves." Finally, the Chairman of the Joint Chiefs of Staff, General Earle Gilmore Wheeler, announced that "there may be a Communist thrust similar to the desperate effort of the Germans in the Battle of the Bulge in World War II."

Thus the American public was wholly unprepared for what was about to happen, and it was soon appreciated as the major turning point of the Vietnam War.

Glossary

Aircraft carrier The type of warship that took over from the battleship as the world's most important type of capital ship during World War II. It is in essence a floating airfield with provision for hangaring, maintaining, and operating a substantial number of aircraft.

Armored personnel carrier A vehicle designed to move troops on the battlefield. It is generally a tracked vehicle that provides the embarked men protection against small arms fire; the troops are generally carried in a compartment at the rear of the vehicle accessed, in the case of the American M113, by a powered rear ramp/door.

Artillery An overall term for tube weapons that fire shells rather than bullets, and which are too large and complex to be operated by an individual soldier.

Battalion A basic subdivision of the regiment, generally less than 1,000 men and commanded by a lieutenant colonel.

Blockade A naval and/or air campaign to deny the enemy or neutrals access to or departure from the enemy's ports and coast.

Bomber An airplane designed to deliver free-fall bombs, therefore a comparatively large type with greater range than the fighter. It generally carries its offensive weapons in a lower-fuselage bomb bay and is fitted with defensive gun turrets to deal with enemy fighters.

Brigade The basic subdivision of a division, generally containing two or more battalions and commanded by a brigadier general.

Company The basic subdivision of a battalion, generally less than 200 men and commanded by a captain. The cavalry equivalent is the troop.

Corps A primary component of the army containing two or more divisions. A corps is commanded in the U.S. Army by a major general, but in most other armies by a lieutenant general.

Destroyer A warship intermediate in size and capability between a frigate and a cruiser. The type is one of any navy's "workhorse" vessels which combines affordability with high performance, and it is large enough to carry a useful sensor and weapon load.

Division The smallest army formation, including two or more brigades and commanded by a major general. It is the basic organization designed for independent operation and therefore contains support elements (artillery, engineers, etc.) in addition to its infantry.

Formation Any large body of troops organized for operations independent of the rest of the army. It therefore possesses, in addition to its organic infantry units, a full complement of artillery, engineer, and support services. The smallest formation is generally the division.

Gun One of the basic weapons of the artillery. It is a high-velocity weapon with a comparatively long barrel designed for the direct engagement (firing at an elevation angle below 45°) of targets that can be seen through the weapon's sight.

Howitzer One of the basic weapons of the artillery. It is a low-velocity weapon with a comparatively short barrel, designed for the indirect engagement (firing at an elevation angle of more than 45°) of targets hidden from direct sight by some intervening feature.

Logistics The science of planning and carrying out the movement of forces and their supplies.

Materiel The overall term for equipment, stores, supplies, and spares.

Regiment A basic tactical unit, subordinate to the brigade and made up of two or more battalions under the command of a colonel.

Mine An explosive device generally encased in metal or plastic and designed to destroy or incapacitate vehicles, or to kill or wound personnel. The two basic types of mine are the land mine, a comparatively small weapon which is usually buried in the ground, and the sea mine, a considerably larger weapon either laid on the bottom of shallow waters or, in deeper waters, floating just below the surface at the top of an anchored cable.

Mortar A light tube weapon, made up of a barrel, supporting leg(s), and a baseplate. It can be broken down into sections to be hand carried and is designed to fire its bombs on a high trajectory that ends with an almost vertical descent on the target.

Recoilless rifle An antitank (and antibunker) weapon that generates no recoil as it fires a rocket-powered projectile.

Strategy The art of winning a campaign or war by major operations.

Tactics The art of winning a battle by minor operations.

Unit Any small body of troops not organized with capability for operations independent of the rest of the army. Therefore, it does not possess in addition to its organic infantry units the full range of artillery, engineer, and support services. The largest unit is the regimental combat team, generally known in other armies as the brigade.

Bibliography

Arnold, James R. *Armor.*
(Bantam Books, New York, 1987).
The surprising usefulness of armored fighting vehicles in Vietnam.

Arnold, James R. *Rangers.*
(Bantam Books, New York, 1988).
The specially trained recon forces and superior ARVN Rangers battalions.

Boettcher, Thomas D. *Vietnam: The Valor and the Sorrow.*
(Little, Brown & Co., Boston, 1985).

Broughton, Jack. *Thud Ridge.*
(Bantam Books, New York, 1985).
A pilot's account of aerial combat over North Vietnam.

Brown, Malcolm W. *The New Face of War.*
(Bantam Books, New York, 1986).

Caputo, Philip. *A Rumor of War.*
(Holt Rinehart & Winston, New York, 1977).

Donovan, David. *Once A Warrior King: Memories of an Officer in Vietnam.*
(McGraw-Hill, New York, 1985).
An advisor's story who served in an isolated post in the Delta.

Fall, Bernard. *Street Without Joy.*
(The Stackpole Company, Harrisburg PA, 1967).
Primarily focused on the French in Indochina; essential for understanding what befell the U.S.

Giap, Vo Nguyen. *Big Victory, Great Task.*
(Frederick A. Praeger, New York, 1968).
By the strategic genius behind the North Vietnamese war effort.

Goldman, Peter and Tony Fuller et. al. *Charlie Company: What Vietnam Did to Us.*
(William Morrow & Co., New York, 1983).

Hackworth, David H., and Julie Sherman. *About Face: The Odyssey of an American Warrior.*
(Simon & Schuster, New York, 1989).
The story of the disillusionment of a crack warrior.

Henderson, Charles. *Marine Sniper.*
(Stein & Day, New York, 1986).
The amazing exploits of a master marksman.

Knoebl, Kuno. *Victor Charlie: The Face of War in Vietnam.*
(Frederick A. Praeger, New York, 1967).

Mason, Robert. *Chickenhawk.*
(Penguin Books, New York, 1984).
The helicopter war.

Maurer, Harry. *Strange Ground: Americans in Vietnam 1945-1975.*
(Henry Holt & Co, New York, 1989).
Excellent compilation of oral histories from soldiers at all levels.

Oberdorfer, Don. *Tet!*
(Doubleday & Co., Garden City, NY, 1971).

Santoli, Al. *Everything We Had: An Oral History of the Vietnam War by Thirty-Three American Soldiers Who Fought There.*
(Random House, New York, 1981).
Excellent compilation of first-hand accounts.

Sheehan, Neil. *A Bright Shining Lie.*
(Random House, New York, 1988).
A massive, detailed account about a very influential American adviser to South Vietnam.

Stanton, Shelby L. *Anatomy of a Division: 1st Cav in Vietnam.*
(Presidio Press, Novato, CA, 1987).
An organizational and battle history of the world's first air cavalry division.

Summers, Col. Harry G., Jr. *On Strategy: The Vietnam War in Context.*
(U.S. Army War College, Carlisle, PA, 1981).
A controversial description of what went wrong, focusing on the strategic level.

Walt, Lewis W. *Strange War, Strange Strategy: A General's Report on Vietnam.*
(Funk & Wagnalls, New York, 1970).
A respected Marine Corps general's war memoirs.

Westmoreland, Gen. William C. *A Soldier Reports.*
(Doubleday & Co., Garden City, NY, 1976).
Top American commander's war memoirs.

Index

Page numbers in *Italics* refer to illustration